Science

FOR COMMON ENTRANCE

13+

Exam Practice Questions

Science

FOR COMMON ENTRANCE

13+

Exam Practice Questions

Ron Pickering

GALORE PARK

AN HACHETTE UK COMPANY

About the author

Ron Pickering has published a number of very successful books covering GCSE, IGCSE and A-level syllabuses and has worked in both maintained and independent education for more than 30 years. He now divides his time between teacher training, both in the UK and overseas, and writing. Ron has been a science advisor and curriculum manager at Altrincham Grammar School for Girls, as well as a Science Inspector for OFSTED.

Acknowledgements

I dedicate this book to all young scientists, wherever they are, but especially to two microscientists, Noah and Kay, our beloved grandsons.

Every effort has been made to trace all copyright holders, but if any have been inadvertently overlooked, the Publishers will be pleased to make the necessary arrangements at the first opportunity.

Although every effort has been made to ensure that website addresses are correct at time of going to press, Galore Park cannot be held responsible for the content of any website mentioned in this book. It is sometimes possible to find a relocated web page by typing in the address of the home page for a website in the URL window of your browser.

Hachette UK's policy is to use papers that are natural, renewable and recyclable products and made from wood grown in sustainable forests. The logging and manufacturing processes are expected to conform to the environmental regulations of the country of origin.

Orders: please contact Bookpoint Ltd, 130 Milton Park, Abingdon, Oxon OX14 4SB. Telephone: (44) 01235 827720. Fax: (44) 01235 400454. Email education@bookpoint.co.uk. Lines are open from 9 a.m. to 5 p.m., Monday to Saturday, with a 24-hour message answering service. Visit our website at www.galorepark.co.uk for details of other revision guides for Common Entrance, examination papers and Galore Park publications.

ISBN: 978 1 4718 4719 6

© Ron Pickering 2015

First published in 2015 by
Galore Park Publishing Ltd,
An Hachette UK Company
Carmelite House
50 Victoria Embankment
London EC4Y 0DZ
www.galorepark.co.uk

Impression number   10 9 8 7 6
Year   2019

The following illustrations are by Aptara, Inc.: p22(t), p22(m), p23, p25, p32(m), p32(b), p33, p44(m), p44(b), p49, p50(m), p61(b), p62(t), p118, p121(m), p126(m), p129(t), p133(b), p136

All other illustrations are by Ian Moores and are re-used with permission.

Typeset in India by Aptara, Inc.
Printed and bound by CPI Group (UK) Ltd, Croydon, CR0 4YY

A catalogue record for this title is available from the British Library.

Contents

Introduction

Science for Common Entrance 13+ Exam Practice Questions is a book of sample exercises for Common Entrance preparation, based on the ISEB syllabus for Science.

Unlike a Common Entrance exam paper, each chapter of the book tests a single topic. The aim of this structure is to allow you to focus on the topics in which you feel you are weakest, reinforcing your understanding of key terms, as well as your knowledge of the relevant natural forces and processes.

Just as in the Common Entrance papers, each section begins with a series of multiple-choice questions. These questions will very quickly tell you whether you know the basics of the test topic. The questions include a variety of styles typical of Common Entrance examinations at both level 1 and level 2.

It is recommended that students who score less than 40% overall on these papers should consider using the Level 1 paper.

→ Timing

Try to complete each test within 40 minutes, which is the time allocated to each Level 2 exam paper. Do not count the time you spend copying graphs or tables.

If you are entitled to extra time, use it according to the advice from your teacher.

→ Drawing graphs

You should write all of your answers on separate paper (not in the book), and this includes drawing graphs. Where a graph is provided in the book, copy it (including axes, numbers and labels) onto appropriate graph paper and draw points and lines as required.

→ Calculations

CE papers require you to show your working when you answer a numerical question. This can be very helpful, as you may be awarded marks for working even if your final answer is incorrect.

→ Straight lines

Use a ruler to draw straight lines, for example when drawing rays of light or putting a border on a table of results.

→ Your exams at 13+

Assessment of the 13+ syllabus can occur at two levels: Level 1 and Level 2. The syllabus is common for both levels. Candidates who are expected to achieve less than an average of 40% on the three Level 2 papers should consider using the Level 1 paper.

Level 1 (80 marks; 60 minutes)

There will be one paper with approximately equal numbers of questions based on the 13+ biology, chemistry and physics syllabuses. The paper will consist of a mixture of closed items, for example multiple choice, matching pairs, completing sentences and some open questions. Open questions will have several parts, some of which will require answers of one or two sentences. These parts will carry a maximum of 3 marks. At least 25% of the paper will be testing *Working Scientifically*.

For questions that require the use of formulae, equations will be provided. Rearrangement of equations will not be required.

There will be no choice of questions. The use of calculators and protractors will be allowed in the examination.

Level 2 (60 marks; 40 minutes)

There will be three papers, one in each of biology, chemistry and physics. Some of the questions may be closed, although most will be open with several parts requiring candidates to answer in sentences. These parts will carry a maximum of 4 marks. In addition, 1 mark may be given for an acceptable standard of spelling, punctuation and grammar in one part of the paper. The maximum number of marks per question will be 12. At least 25% of the paper will be testing *Working Scientifically*

There will be no choice of questions. The use of calculators and protractors will be allowed in the examination.

For quantitative questions that require the use of formulae, equations given in the syllabus will *not* be provided.

Scholarship

Scholarship papers are based on this syllabus. The Common Academic Scholarship Examination (90 minutes, including 10 minutes of reading time) will be divided into three sections: A (Biology), B (Chemistry) and C (Physics). Candidates will be required to attempt all questions. Each section is worth 25 marks but the number of questions will vary. The use of calculators and protractors will be allowed in the examination.

For quantitative questions that require the use of formulae, equations given in the syllabus will *not* be provided. Rearrangement of equations may be required.

→ Command words

Make sure you completely understand these words and phrases. Cover up the definitions with a sheet of paper in order to test yourself.

annotate	add descriptive, explanatory labels
choose	select carefully from a number of alternatives
complete	finish, make whole
define	give an exact description of; just a formal statement is required
describe	write down the main points of the feature; note that this does *not* include an explanation
develop	expand upon an idea
explain	write in detail how something has come into being and/or changed; answers will usually include the word 'because'
give	show evidence of
identify	find evidence in information supplied as part of the questions (often a table or a diagram)
list	put a number of examples in sequence
mark and name	show the exact location of, and add the name
name	give a precise example of
select	pick out as most suitable or best; this is effectively the same command as 'choose'
state	give a concise answer with little or no supporting evidence; this could be a statement in words or a numerical answer
study	look at and/or read carefully
suggest	propose reasons or ideas for something; there may be no unique answer, but you are being asked to provide an answer from your scientific or general knowledge

These words are only used in the scholarship exam:

discuss   present viewpoints from various aspects of a subject
elaborate   similar to expand and illustrate
expand   develop an argument and/or present greater detail on
illustrate   use examples to develop an argument or theme

→ Know what to expect in the examination

- Use past papers to familiarise yourself with the format of the exam.
- Make sure you understand the language examiners use.

→ Before the examination

- Have all your equipment and pens ready the night before.
- Make sure you are at your best by getting a good night's sleep before the exam.
- Have a good breakfast in the morning.
- Take some water into the exam if you are allowed.
- Think positively and keep calm.

→ During the examination

- Have a watch on your desk. Work out how much time you need to allocate to each question and try to stick to it.
- Make sure you read and understand the instructions and rules on the front of the exam paper.
- Allow some time at the start to read and consider the questions carefully before writing anything.
- Read all the questions at least twice. Don't rush into answering before you have a chance to think about it.
- If a question is particularly hard move on to the next one. Go back to it if you have time at the end.
- Always look on the back of the paper because there might be questions there that you have not answered.
- Check your answers make sense if you have time at the end.

→ Tips for the science examination

- You should write your answers on the question paper; you may use a calculator and remember *all* questions should be attempted.
- Look at the number of marks allocated for each question in order to assess how many relevant points are required for a full answer. Very often, marks are awarded for giving your reasons for writing a particular answer.
- In numerical questions, workings out should be shown and the correct units used.

- Practical skills are important. Look back in your lab notes to remind yourself about why you carried out any practical work. What were you trying to find out? What did you actually do? What instrument did you use to take any measurements and what units did you use? How did you record your results: tables, bar charts or graphs? What were the results of your investigation and did you make any plans to change or improve what you did? These are all important and will be tested in the examination.

- A thorough understanding of your practical work will also help you to remember the key facts by putting them into context.

- Neat handwriting and careful presentation may help to put the examiner in a more generous frame of mind!

1 Cells and organisation

1 Which option best completes each of the following sentences?

(a) Respiration is _____ (1)

producing offspring   taking in nutrients

releasing energy   responding to stimuli

(b) Diffusion is _____ (1)

taking in nutrients

movement of particles from high to low concentration

movement of water from outside a cell to inside a cell

movement of gases, liquids and solids

(c) The human male gamete is a _____ (1)

liver cell   sperm cell

pollen grain   nerve cell

(d) Reproduction is _____ (1)

producing offspring   taking in nutrients

releasing energy   increasing in size

(e) Nutrition is _____ (1)

producing offspring   taking in nutrients

releasing energy   responding to stimuli

(f) The basic unit of life is _____ (1)

a molecule   a tissue

an organ   a cell

(g) A collection of cells with the same function is _____ (1)

an organism   a tissue

an organ   a system

(h) the structure inside the cell that carries out aerobic respiration
is the _____ (1)

nucleus   mitochondrion

cytoplasm   chloroplast

(i) a useful stain for observing the nucleus in a cell is _____ (1)

    iodine solution   universal indicator solution

    Benedict's solution   methylene blue

2   The human body contains several different systems. The systems are made up of organs working together so that the body is at its most efficient.

This is a list of some of the organs of the human body. Copy and complete the table below to match the organs listed to the system they belong to. (5)

Teeth   Stomach   Testes

Rib   Heart   Lungs

System	Organs in this system
Digestive	
Circulatory	
Reproductive	
Breathing	
Skeletal	

3   The diagrams below show six cells. One of these cells transports oxygen in the blood. This cell does not contain a nucleus.

A

B
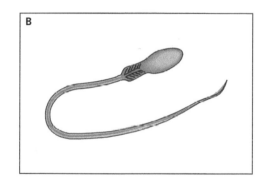

C
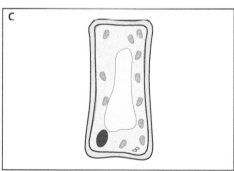

D
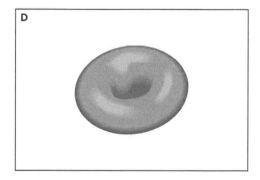

E
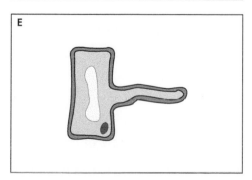

F
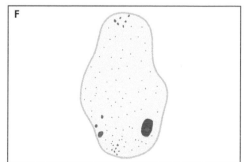

(a) (i) Give the letter of the cell that transports oxygen in the blood (1)

(ii) What is the function of the nucleus in most cells? (1)

(b) Give the letter of the cell that carries genetic information from father to offspring. (1)

(c) Give the letters of **two** plant cells. (2)

(d) Give the letter of the cell with a surface adapted for the uptake of minerals. (1)

4 The diagram shows a plant cell.

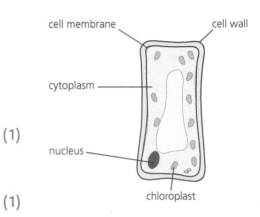

(a) (i) This cell is from the leaf of a sycamore tree. Name the part that is present in this cell but would not be present in a root cell from a sycamore tree. (1)

(ii) Why is the part you have chosen in part (i) not present in a root cell? (1)

(b) The parts labelled in this diagram have different functions. Copy and complete the table below to link each part to its correct function. (5)

Part of cell	Function
	Helps keep the cell shape
	Controls the entry and exit of substances
	Contains the genetic material that controls the cell's activities
	Many chemical reactions take place here
	The site of the trapping of light for photosynthesis

5 (a) One function of cells lining the human trachea (windpipe) is to _____ (1)

sweep away particles of dust

release waste carbon dioxide

secrete mucus to trap microorganisms and particles of dust

absorb oxygen for respiration

(b) A cell with a nucleus, a cell wall and a large surface area for absorption is a _____ (1)

red blood cell   leaf cell

sperm cell   root hair cell

(c) _____ is **not** an example of diffusion. (1)

the movement of food molecules from the intestines to the blood

the movement of oxygen from air sac to blood

the trapping of bacteria by white blood cells

the movement of oxygen out of leaf cells to the atmosphere

6 (a) The diagram below shows a plant cell and an animal cell.

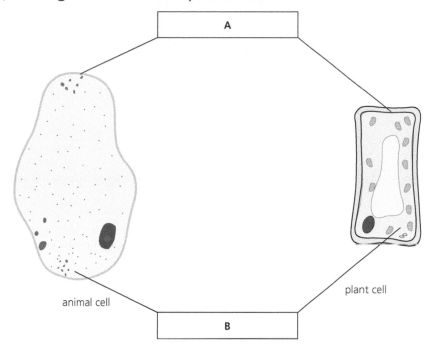

animal cell

plant cell

(I)   Give the names of **two** parts that are present in plant cells but not in animal cells. (2)

(ii) Give the function of **one** of the parts you have named and say why it is important in the life of the plant. (2)

(iii) The letters, A and B, and guidelines show two parts that are present in both plant and animal cells. Identify the two parts and state the function of each of them. (4)

(b) (i) Cells can become **specialised**. What does this word mean? (1)

(ii) Tissues carry out their functions because of the specialised cells they contain. Copy the words in the boxes below and then link together the cells, their special functions and the biological process they are involved in. The first cell has been done as an example. (4)

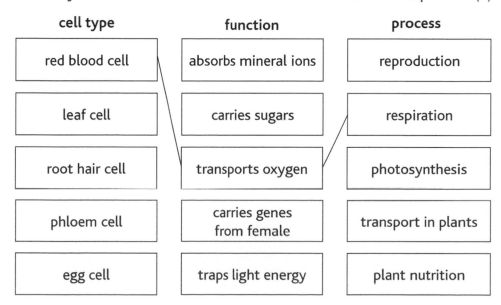

cell type	function	process
red blood cell	absorbs mineral ions	reproduction
leaf cell	carries sugars	respiration
root hair cell	transports oxygen	photosynthesis
phloem cell	carries genes from female	transport in plants
egg cell	traps light energy	plant nutrition

7 The diagram shows a single-celled
organism called *Chlamydomonas*.
This organism is able to swim about
in the small puddles of water where
it lives.

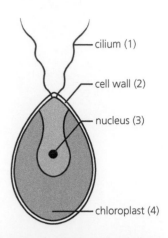

cilium (1)

cell wall (2)

nucleus (3)

chloroplast (4)

(a) In this table, which set of numbers
(A, B, C or D) correctly relates
functions of cell parts to the
structures labelled in the
diagram? (2)

	Function			
	Protection against bursting	Photosynthesis	Movement	Control of cell activities
A	2	4	1	3
B	1	3	2	4
C	4	2	1	3
D	2	4	3	1

(b) Name **three** structures in the *Chlamydomonas* cell that would not be
found in a sperm cell. (3)

Nutrition and digestion

1   Which option best completes each of the following sentences?

(a) The most important food for muscle growth and repair
is _____

(1)

fat   carbohydrate

calcium   protein

(b) Brussels sprouts are a good source of _____

(1)

fat   vitamin D

sugar   fibre

(c) Most digested food enters the blood in the _____

(1)

stomach   liver

small intestine   kidney

(d) Iodine solution is a stain used to detect _____

(1)

protein   sugar

fat   starch

(e) Calcium is essential in a balanced diet to _____

(1)

prevent scurvy   help develop strong bones

supply energy   help digestion

(f) Egg whites are a good source of _____

(1)

sugar   protein

fat   starch

(g) The most important teeth for biting off pieces of an apple are
the _____

(1)

molars   canines

pre-molars   incisors

(h) A positive result in Benedict's test shows the presence
of _____

(1)

starch   an acid

sugar   water

(i) The teeth used by a tiger to kill its prey are the _____ (1)

incisors	premolars
molars	canines

2 Ferdinand Magellan led the first voyage around the world. He sailed from Spain in 1519, hoping to find a new route to the Spice Islands.

There were five ships in his small convoy, with 237 men. Each ship carried a supply of basic foods including flour, cheese, dry biscuits, oil, meat and vegetables. The ships arrived at the Spice Islands after a difficult voyage of 20 months, but only one was able to return to Spain. The sailors on this ship became very ill before they reached Spain again – they had sores that would not heal and their teeth fell out of their bleeding gums.

One sailor, named Elcarno, ate a spoonful of fruit jam every day and he did not develop any of these symptoms.

(a) The mixture of foods taken by Magellan's ships did not provide a **balanced diet**. What is meant by a balanced diet? (2)

(b) The sailors developed a deficiency disease called scurvy on the return voyage to Spain.

   (i) What is meant by a **deficiency disease**? (1)

   (ii) What is the cause of scurvy? (1)

   (iii) Describe one symptom of scurvy. (1)

   (iv) Suggest why the sailor Elcarno did **not** develop this deficiency disease. (1)

   (v) Name one other food that would reduce the risk of developing scurvy. (1)

3 (a) Poor diet can lead to bad health. Draw lines to match up each fact about the diet to the harm it may cause. (3)

fact about diet	harm caused
too much salt	constipation
too little iron	high blood pressure
too much fat	slow growth of muscles
not enough fibre	cannot carry enough oxygen in blood
too little protein	heart disease

(b) A properly balanced diet should help to prevent this harm. Link each of these components of a balanced diet to its function in a healthy body. (3)

component of diet | function in a healthy body

| sugar |

| required for development of bones and teeth |

| calcium |

| an important part of the process of digesting foods |

| vitamin C |

| the main source of energy for working cells |

| water |

| provides a slow, steady supply of sugar |

| starch |

| prevents scurvy |

4 The table below provides information about five different foods.

Food	Energy content in kJ per 100 g	Nutrients (per 100 g)			
		Carbohydrate (g)	Fat (g)	Protein (g)	Calcium (mg)
Yoghurt	280	5.0	4.0	3.0	120
Cheese	1700	0.2	35.2	24.0	710
Pear	380	26.1	0.1	0.8	6
Brown Rice	900	42.7	1.8	9.5	64
Butter	3118	0	82.1	0.4	17

(a) (i) Which of the nutrients provides most of the energy in the brown rice? (1)

(ii) Which of the four nutrients provides insulation against cold? (1)

(iii) Which of the foods would be most useful to a weightlifter needing to build his muscles? (1)

(b) (i) What is the total amount of the three nutrients, fat, protein and carbohydrate, in yoghurt? (1)

(ii) What makes up most of the rest of the 100 g of yoghurt? (1)

(c) (i) A teenage boy needs about 9000 kJ of energy every day. How much brown rice would he need to eat to obtain this amount of energy? (1)

(ii) The boy also needs about 55 g of protein every day. Would this same amount of rice provide all of his protein requirements? (1)

(d) The table below shows the recommended daily amount (RDA) of calcium for a female at different times in her life.

Stage of life cycle	RDA of calcium in mg
Baby aged 3 months	450
12-year-old girl	900
21-year-old, non-pregnant woman	550
Pregnant woman	1200
Breast-feeding woman	

(i) Suggest what would be the RDA of calcium for a breast-feeding woman. Explain your answer. (1)

(ii) Explain why the 12-year-old girl has a higher RDA of calcium than the 21-year-old woman. (1)

(iii) The 21-year-old woman needs only about three-quarters of the protein as the 12-year-old girl. Why do we need protein in our diet? (1)

5 Teeth develop properly only if the diet contains plenty of _____ (1)

starch   vitamin C

calcium   iron

6 This diagram shows the digestive system in a human.

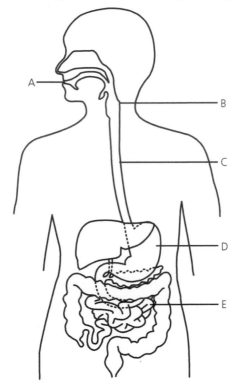

(a) (i) Which letter labels the part where the incisors and canines are found? (1)

(ii) Proteins are digested to amino acids. How are the amino acids carried to other parts of the body? (1)

(b) Scientists are sure that a healthy diet reduces the risk of disease. They often recommend certain foods to improve health – for example, foods low in cholesterol are known to reduce the risk of heart disease. One of these recommended foods is mycoprotein, an artificial 'meat' made from the bodies of harmless fungi.

The bar chart shows the levels of different nutrients in beef and in mycoprotein.

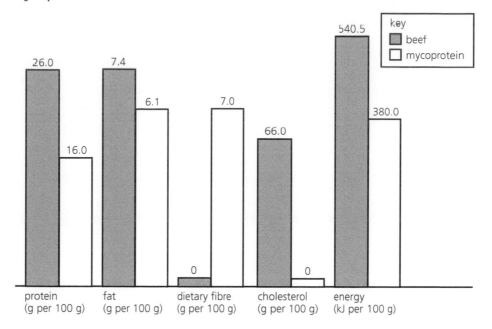

(i) Explain **three** reasons why mycoprotein is healthier than beef. (3)

(ii) Give **two** reasons why it might be better to eat beef than mycoprotein. (2)

(c) The scientists also recommend that we eat more fibre in our diet. They have compared the intake of fibre with the chance of developing colon cancer (the colon is part of the large intestine). This scatter graph shows their results.

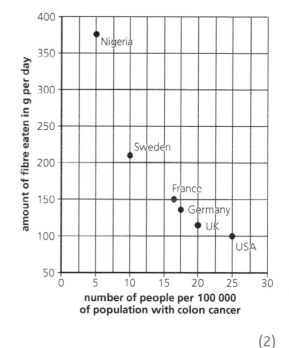

(i) Which country had the largest proportion of people with colon cancer? (1)

(ii) How much more likely is a person in the UK to have colon cancer than one from Nigeria? Explain how you reached your answer. (2)

(iii) Which **two** of the following foods are good sources of fibre? (1)

wholemeal bread   chocolate

cheese   apples

eggs   pizza

7 Sally investigated the pH of milk left in a sealed container for five days. She obtained the following results:

Time in days	pH of sealed milk sample
0	7.1
1	6.4
2	5.9
3	5.2
4	4.5
5	4.1

(a) Plot these results on a graph grid like the one below. (3)

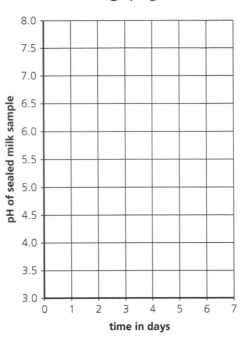

(b) Sally believed that bacteria were causing this change in pH. What were the bacteria releasing to bring about this change? (1)

(c) Use the graph to predict the likely pH after 7 days. (1)

(d) Sally decided to try to find out whether heating the milk would stop this pH change. Describe in detail how she could do this. Use the terms **independent variable**, **dependent variable** and **controlled variable** in your answer. (4)

(e) Humans use this information on the effect of bacteria on milk in many ways. Name **one** food that humans use that is made by letting bacteria turn milk sour. (1)

(f) If we wish to prevent milk from going sour there are many things we can do to it. Choose **two** treatments from this list that would help to prevent milk from going sour. (1)

• Keep the milk at a low temperature in a refrigerator.
• Mix the milk with fruit juice.
• Dry the milk and store it as granules.
• Always shake the milk before pouring it.

For **one** of your choices, explain why the treatment will stop the milk from going sour. (1)

3 Respiration, energy and exercise

1 Which option best completes each of the following sentences?

(a) The skeleton does **not** _____ (1)

support the body   digest foods containing calcium

protect soft internal organs   provide attachment for muscles

(b) Gas exchange in humans takes place in the _____ (1)

windpipe/trachea   liver

alveoli/air sacs   mouth

(c) A gas that turns limewater milky is _____ (1)

oxygen   carbon dioxide

carbon monoxide   water vapour

(d) The gas required by respiring cells is _____ (1)

carbon dioxide   water vapour

nitrogen   oxygen

(e) Cigarette smoking does **not** cause harm to the _____ (1)

lungs   fingernails

heart   unborn baby

(f) The release of energy by the oxidation of food is _____ (1)

digestion   absorption

excretion   respiration

(g) The normal resting pulse rate in a healthy individual
is approximately _____ (1)

40 bpm   120 bpm

70 bpm   100 bpm

(h) Respiration does not release _____ (1)

carbon dioxide   heat

water   glucose

(i) a condition in which restricted breathing can be treated by an inhaler is _____ (1)

| asthma | tiredness after exercise |
| lung cancer | accidental swallowing of a fizzy drink |

2 The diagram shows the rib cage in a human.

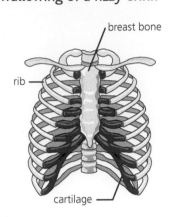

(a) The rib cage is able to move during breathing.

(i) Which type of tissue is responsible for this movement? (1)

(ii) In which direction do the ribs move when we breathe in? (1)

(b) The rib cage also plays a part in protecting delicate organs. Give the names of **two** organs that the rib cage protects. (2)

(c) There are other sets of bones involved in movement. This diagram shows the bones of the human arm.

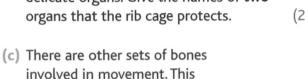

(i) State the name of the muscle that contracts to **straighten** the arm? (1)

(ii) State the name of the muscle that contracts to **bend** the arm? (1)

(iii) The muscles make up a pair. One of them relaxes while the other one is contracting. What is the scientific name for this kind of pairing? (1)

3 David wanted to compare the energy value of several foods. He used the apparatus shown below and measured the rise in temperature caused by the burning food sample.

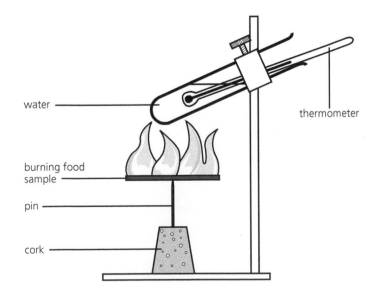

(a) (i)   What is the **independent** (input) **variable** in his experiment?   (1)

(ii)   What is the **dependent** (outcome) **variable** in his experiment?   (1)

(iii) Suggest **two** steps that David should take to make this a fair test.   (2)

(iv) David's teacher suggested collecting all of the class results together before trying to draw conclusions. Why is this important?   (2)

(b) (i)   In a living cell the food does not burn in this way to release energy. What is the name of the process that releases energy from foods in living cells?   (1)

(ii)   Give **two** reasons why energy is required in the body.   (2)

4   (a) When cigarette smoke is bubbled through universal indicator solution, the solution changes from _____   (1)

red to yellow   blue to green

green to red/orange   green to blue

(b) Muscles that help in breathing are _____   (1)

biceps and triceps   intercostals and diaphragm

diaphragm and biceps   intercostals and triceps

(c) Anaerobic respiration in animals produces _____   (1)

glucose   some energy and carbon dioxide

alcohol and carbon dioxide   lactic acid and some energy

5   Anika was a good athlete and wanted to find out how training was affecting her breathing. She was able to use a machine that measures the volume of air breathed in and out – the machine allows measurements to be made **before** and **during** exercise.

(a) The chart shows results obtained during one investigation.

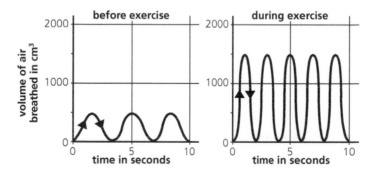

(i)   How much more air did Anika breathe in with each breath during exercise (in cm³)?   (1)

(ii)   The air contains 20% oxygen. How much more **oxygen** did Anika breathe in per **minute**? Show your working.   (4)

(iii) Copy and complete this word equation to explain why Anika breathed in this extra oxygen during the period of exercise.   (2)

_____ + oxygen ⟶ _____ + water + _____

15

(b) Which other organ in Anika's body would work faster to help this extra oxygen reach the parts of the body where it is needed? (1)

(c) Sometimes an athlete exercises so hard that not enough oxygen can be obtained. Under these circumstances respiration becomes anaerobic.

 (i) State **two** reasons why this form of respiration is less valuable to the athlete. (2)

 (ii) Anaerobic respiration can also occur in other organisms. Name one organism that can carry out anaerobic respiration to make a product useful to humans. What is this useful product? (2)

6 The diagram below shows part of a human breathing system.

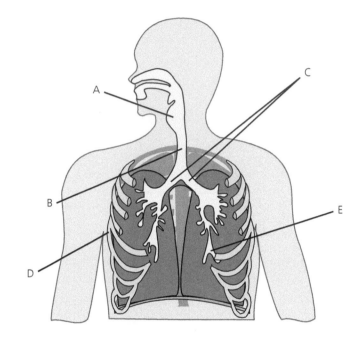

(a) Give the letters that label:

 (i) the part that protects the lungs (1)

 (ii) the part where gases are exchanged between blood and air (1)

 (iii) Carbon monoxide damages the cells lining the windpipe, and tar irritates these cells so that they make more mucus. Suggest a result of this for a cigarette smoker? (2)

(b) (i) Which gas passes from air to blood in the part you have identified in (a) (ii)? (1)

 (ii) Which gas passes from blood to air? (1)

 (iii) What is the name of the process that moves the particles of these gases? (1)

 (iv) The lining that these gases cross is **thin** and with a **large surface area**. Explain why each of these features is important. (2)

Reproduction in humans

1 Which option best completes each of the following sentences?

(a) The human male gamete is _____ (1)

an ovum	a sperm
an antibody	a zygote

(b) A young woman ovulates every _____ (1)

3 weeks	28 weeks
28 days	3 months

(c) The process when gametes join together is called _____ (1)

ovulation	menstruation
gestation	fertilisation

(d) Sperm are produced in the _____ (1)

sperm duct	scrotum
testis	penis

(e) The genes from the two parents are carried in the part of the sex cell called the _____ (1)

cytoplasm	nucleus
membrane	embryo

(f) The stage of human development at which a person becomes able to reproduce is called _____ (1)

adulthood	activity
gestation	adolescence

(g) Two sex cells join together to form _____ (1)

an embryo	a fetus
a zygote	a gamete

(h) The part of the body where substances can be exchanged between a pregnant woman and her developing baby is the _____ (1)

liver	placenta
umbilical cord	amniotic sac

(i) The length of time between fertilisation and birth is called _____ (1)

gestation   menstruation

conception   copulation

2   The diagram shows the reproductive system of a male.

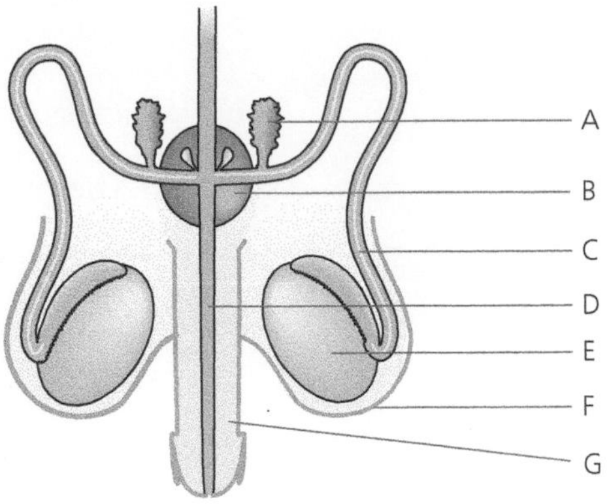

(a) Which of the labelled structures (choose the correct letter in each case):

(i)   produces sperm?   (1)

(ii) carries urine as well as sperm?   (1)

(iii) produces a fluid for sperm to swim in?   (1)

(b) (i) Which structure, shown in the diagram, is cut in a common contraceptive operation?   (1)

(ii) Explain why this operation is a successful form of contraception.   (1)

(c) A chemical called testosterone is produced in a boy's body from adolescence onwards. This chemical causes certain changes in the boy's body.

Describe **two** changes caused by testosterone.   (2)

3   This diagram shows a fetus in the uterus just before birth.

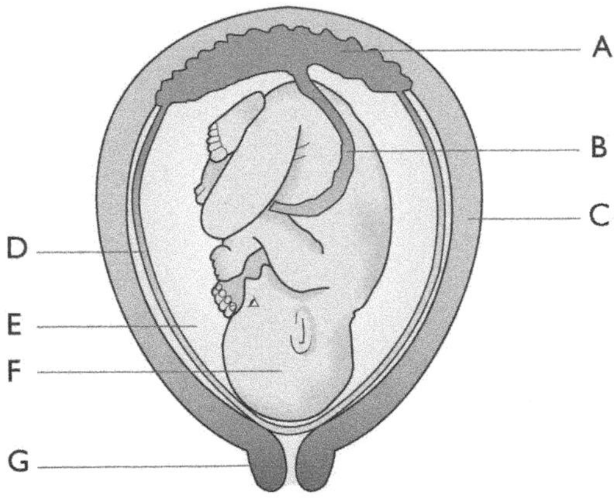

(a) Which letter labels:

(i)   the amniotic sac?   (1)

(ii) the umbilical cord?   (1)

(iii) a muscle that can push out the baby at birth?   (1)

(b) What is the normal length of pregnancy in humans in months?   (1)

(c) What is the function of the amniotic fluid around the fetus?   (1)

(d) The pregnant woman sometimes has cravings for particular foods. Many women like to have milk chocolate, which contains a lot of sugar. Explain in detail how this sugar reaches the developing fetus while the fetus is inside its mother's uterus?   (4)

4 The diagrams below show some cells.

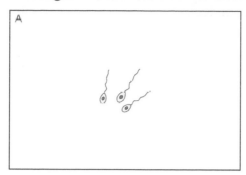 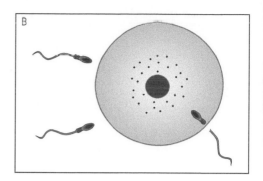

(a) (i) What is the name of cell A? (1)

 (ii) Give **two** ways in which this cell is adapted to its function. (2)

(b) (i) What process is shown in B? (1)

 (ii) Where does this process take place? (1)

(c) Copy and complete the following sentences. (4)

About six days after process B occurs a ball of cells called an
_____ becomes embedded in the thickened wall of the
_____. This process is called _____, and once
it has successfully been completed a new structure called the
_____ forms, linking the mother to her developing baby.

5 This question is about the menstrual cycle.

(a) Copy and complete the following sentences. (5)

One of the _____ releases an egg cell (ovum) every
_____. If there is no fertilisation, or the fertilised egg does
not stick to the lining of the womb, then _____ occurs.
When this process takes place, a woman loses _____. This is
often called 'having a _____'.

(b) This diagram shows the lining of the uterus during the menstrual cycle.

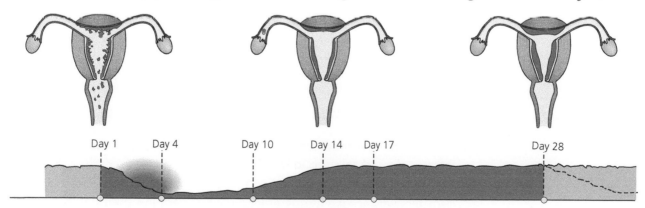

Between or around which days is the time:

(i) of ovulation? (1)

(ii) when the uterus lining is lost? (1)

(iii) when fertilisation is most likely? (1)

6 During pregnancy a woman's body undergoes many changes. One noticeable change is that her body swells as the fetus grows. This table shows the changes in mass of some of her body parts. Answer the questions below.

Body part	Increase in mass in kg
Uterus	1.0
Breast tissue	0.4
Fat	3.7
Placenta	0.7
Blood	0.4
Amniotic fluid	0.8

(a) (i) Use the figures in the table to plot a bar chart on a grid like the one below. Do **not** include the figure for fat in your bar chart. (3)

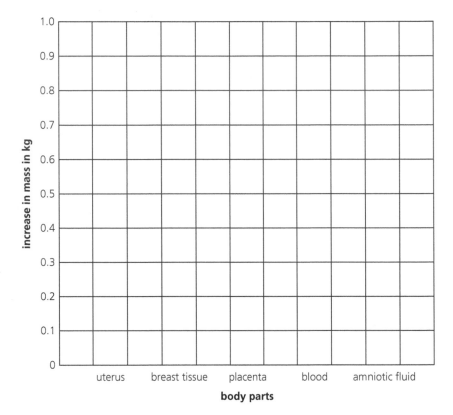

(ii) The mother also gains about 1.5 kg of water and about 0.5 kg of bone. Calculate the total gain in mass, including the figure for fat, during pregnancy. (1)

(iii) What proportion of this gain in mass is due to the placenta? Show your working. (2)

(b) Explain why the pregnant woman must make sure that she has plenty of **protein** and **calcium** in her diet. (2)

(c) Mothers who smoke during pregnancy risk harming their babies. Tobacco smoke contains many chemicals, including **nicotine** and **carbon monoxide gas** (this gas combines with red blood cells and reduces their capacity to transport oxygen).

Explain how these might cause damage to the developing fetus. (2)

Reproduction in plants

1 Which option best completes each of the following sentences? (6)

(a) The anther of a flower _____ (1)

    receives pollen   attracts insects

    produces pollen   holds up the stigma

(b) The male sex cell in a pollen grain contains _____ (1)

    a food supply for the new plant

    half of the chromosomes from a male plant cell

    half of the chromosomes from a female plant cell

    all of the chromosomes from a male plant cell

(c) The male sex cell in a pollen grain does not have _____ (1)

    a membrane   cytoplasm

    a nucleus   chloroplasts

(d) A reagent that can be used to test for starch in a seed
is _____ (1)

    universal indicator   limewater

    iodine solution   methylene blue

(e) A plant cell wall is made of _____ (1)

    protein   fat

    starch   cellulose

(f) The part of a flower that receives pollen from a visiting insect is
the _____ (1)

    stigma   anther

    petal   sepal

2 (a) This is a diagram of a single grass flower. Replace the letters A to G with labels chosen from this list. (8)

anther

filament

ovary

pollen grains

stamen

stigma

style

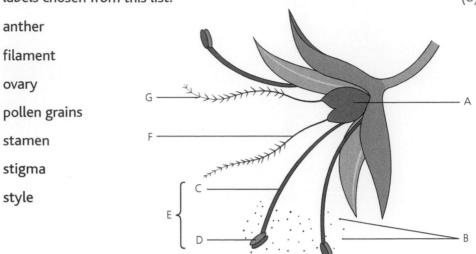

(b) Describe and explain **two** features of this flower that make pollination more likely to be successful. (2)

3 (a) The diagram below shows an experiment on the germination of pea seeds.

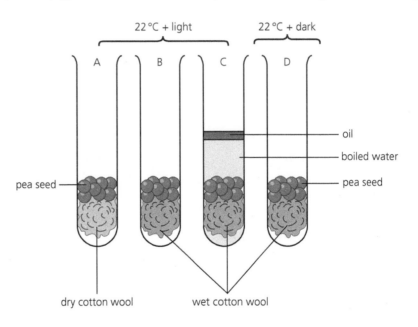

Copy and complete this table. (4)

Tube	Would seeds germinate (write YES or NO)
A	
B	
C	
D	

(b) Sara and Barry measured the dry mass of some germinating barley seedlings for the first 35 days after sowing. Their results are shown in this table.

Time after sowing in days	0	7	14	21	28	35
Dry mass in g	4.0	2.8	2.8	4.4	6.8	8.6

(i) Plot these results in a line graph. (2)

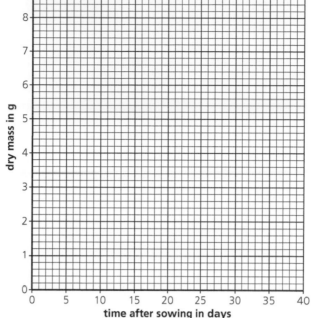

(ii) How many days after sowing did the barley seedlings regain their original mass? (1)

(iii) Explain why the dry mass falls in the first stages of germination. (1)

4 Which option best completes each of the following sentences?

(a) The roots of a small plant grow _____ (1)

towards light and against gravity   with gravity and away from light

towards light and with gravity   towards both light and water

(b) In the plant life cycle, insects are most important for _____ (1)

dispersal   pollination

fertilisation   photosynthesis

(c) The part of the seed that protects it from bacteria and fungi is the _____ (1)

carbohydrate store   micropyle

seed leaf   testa/seed coat

(d) For germination, a seed requires _____ (1)

oxygen, water and light

water, oxygen and a suitable temperature

water, carbon dioxide and a suitable temperature

oxygen, light and a suitable temperature

5 This diagram shows a section through an insect-pollinated flower.

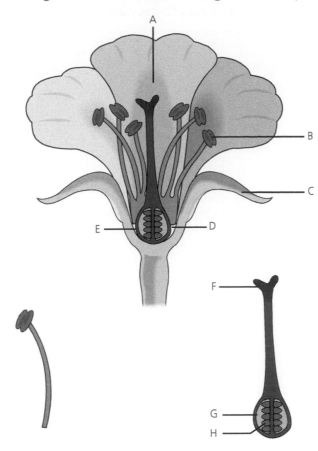

(a) Use the label letters to identify which part of the flower:

    (i)   makes the male sex cells   (1)

    (ii) attracts insects   (1)

    (iii) will eventually become a fruit   (1)

    (iv) receives pollen   (1)

(b) This paragraph is about the life cycle of plants. Copy and complete it by filling in the missing words, chosen from this list.   (5)

dispersal	fertilisation
pollination	germinates
reproduction	grows

A young plant develops when a seed _____ and matures until it produces a flower for _____ . Male gametes are transferred during the process of _____ and join with female gametes during _____ . Eventually fruits are formed, and are separated from the parent plant during the process of _____ .

(c) Jack noticed that birds often eat seeds and his teacher explained that the seeds contained food stores such as starch. Describe in detail how Jack could test that seeds contain starch. Include any control he would need to use and give one safety precaution he should take.   (4)

6 Some lily plants produce heat energy to raise the temperature of their flowers.
   The heat attracts insects to the flower and is released during the process of
   aerobic respiration.

   (a) State *one* benefit to the plant
       of attracting insects.   (1)

   (b) A scientist was interested in the
       relationship between aerobic
       respiration and temperature
       of the flowers. He took 20
       lily flowers and measured the
       temperature and the rate of
       oxygen uptake for each one of
       them. The results are shown in
       the graph:

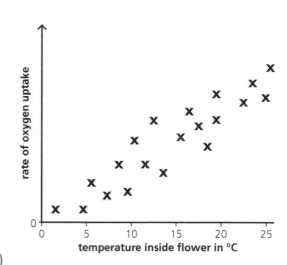

       (i) Describe the relationship
            between the temperature
            inside the flower and the
            rate of oxygen uptake.   (1)

       (ii) Explain the reasons for the
            relationship you have described.   (2)

   (c) (i) What is the fuel used by the lily to produce this heat energy?   (1)

       (ii) Explain how the lilies obtain a supply of this fuel.   (2)

6 Health

1 Which option best completes each of the following sentences?

(a) A disease that can be passed on to another, unrelated person
   is _____ (1)

   infectious   fatal

   inherited   caused by lifestyle

(b) The benefits of exercise do **not** include _____ (1)

   increased stamina   greater strength

   athlete's foot   a stronger heart

(c) When the body cannot function without a drug the person is said
   to be _____ (1)

   acclimatised   activated

   adapted   addicted

(d) An example of an infectious disease is _____ (1)

   lung cancer   heart disease

   influenza   depression

(e) Excessive use of alcohol can cause _____ (1)

   tuberculosis   a cold

   AIDS   liver damage

(f) A medicinal compound that can reduce the growth of bacteria inside the
   body is _____ (1)

   an antiseptic   an antibody

   aspirin   an antibiotic

(g) Fibre is needed in the diet to reduce the risk of _____ (1)

   constipation   liver damage

   brain tumours   weakened bones

(h) The drug marijuana is likely to affect the workings of the _____ (1)

   liver and bones in the rib cage   testes and lungs

   brain and nervous system   liver and testes

2   Doctors have studied the factors that affect heart disease in males in the United Kingdom. Some of their results are shown in this bar chart.

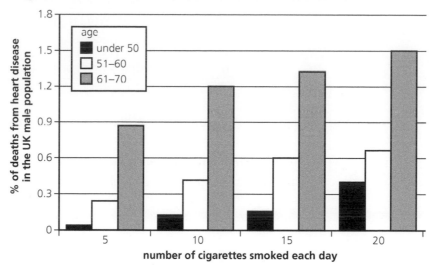

(a) Write **two** conclusions about the effect of smoking on heart disease in males. (2)

(b) This diagram shows the effect of smoking on the arteries of the heart.

healthy artery   artery of smoker

   (i)   Explain how this could cause damage to the heart. (2)

   (ii) Smoking also causes a rise in blood pressure. Explain how this could affect the health of a smoker. (1)

(c) Anna smokes every day. This graph shows the amount of nicotine in her blood after smoking a cigarette. She feels the need for a cigarette once the nicotine level falls below the 'demand threshold'.

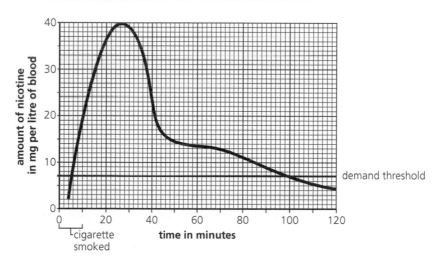

   (i)   How often does Anna need to smoke to keep the nicotine level above the threshold? (1)

   (ii) Suggest why Anna feels anxious and bad-tempered when she wakes up in the morning. (1)

(iii) Smoking 20 cigarettes per day doubles the 'demand threshold'. Where would the new 'demand threshold' be on the graph? (1)

(iv) What effect will this have on the length of time between cigarettes that Anna can wait without becoming stressed? (1)

(v) Suggest **one** other way that Anna can satisfy her craving without smoking a cigarette. (1)

3   Drinking alcohol causes changes in the way the body works.

(a) Copy the words in the boxes below and then draw lines to link the **changes** to the **effects** they have on a drinker's actions and health. (3)

change	effect on actions and health
nerve impulses travel more slowly	poor judgement of distance
blood vessels close to the skin open up	long-term liver damage
senses work less well	person looks red-faced
liver cells try to remove alcohol from blood	reactions are slowed

(b) A pregnant woman can pass any alcohol she drinks to the fetus.

(i)   Describe in detail how the alcohol would reach the fetus. (3)

(ii)   If the woman also smokes she may harm her unborn baby even more. Suggest how chemicals in smoke might affect the health of the unborn baby? (2)

4   Which option best completes each of the following sentences?

(a) A type of medicine that can help defend the body against microbes outside the body is an _____ (1)

antibiotic   aspirin

antiseptic   antibody

(b) A bacterial cell carries its genetic information in its _____ (1)

membrane   DNA

cytoplasm   cell wall

(c) A disease caused by a bacterium is _____ (1)

influenza   athlete's foot

typhoid   AIDS

5 This diagram shows a simple virus.

Viruses reproduce inside living cells and
often cause disease.

protein coat

genetic
material

(a) Name **one** disease caused by a virus. (1)

(b) Complete the following paragraph about disease. Use words from
    this list. (3)

    antibiotic   transfusion

    painkiller   antibody

    vaccination

    Diseases caused by viruses can be prevented by a _____. Following
    this process, the number of _____ molecules in the blood increases. An
    illness caused by a virus cannot be successfully treated with an _____.

6 It is possible to transplant organs into patients suffering from some diseases, such as
   heart failure. A patient who receives a transplanted heart may reject the new heart
   because the immune system recognises the new organ as 'foreign' to the body.

   (a) The patient can take drugs to slow down their immune system.

       Suggest **one** disadvantage to the patient of taking these drugs. (1)

   (b) The patient may also have to take antibiotics following transplant surgery.
       Some of the organisms that might cause infection are resistant to these
       antibiotics. MRSA is the name given to an organism that is resistant to
       many commonly used antibiotics.

       (i) Suggest **two** ways in which MRSA could get into the body of a patient. (2)

       (ii) The nurses looking after the patient are very careful to reduce the risk
            of infections. Explain how the following precautions help to reduce the
            risk of infection.

            • wearing a surgical mask when in the patient's room (1)
            • keeping the windows of the ward closed (1)

   (c) A transplant is less likely to be needed if the heart is healthy. Some aspects
       of our lifestyle can help to protect the heart against disease.

       Underline items from this list that would benefit the heart.

       a diet low in animal fats

       regular exercise

       a diet low in vitamin C

       a diet with twice the normal level of protein

       a lifestyle with little stress

(d) The community is also responsible for fighting disease. Which one of the following is **not** a community responsibility? (1)

- providing safe drinking water
- removal of sewage
- making sure that children have new clothes
- checking on hygienic food preparation

7 Tolani and Fumi ate some soft ice cream on school Sports Day. There were food-poisoning bacteria in the ice cream and they became quite ill the next day. The school doctor gave them antibiotics and told them to take them for 8 days.

This graph shows the change in the number of bacteria in the body if antibiotics are taken.

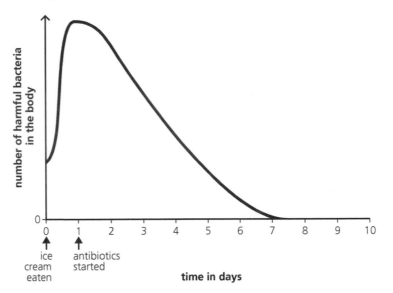

(a) (i) Explain why the sisters did not become unwell until the day after eating the ice cream. (1)

(ii) Tolani felt much better after taking the antibiotics for 8 days. Explain why. (1)

(iii) Fumi is the older sister and thinks she knows better! After 4 days she felt fine and so stopped taking the antibiotics. 2 days later she was really ill again. Explain why this happened. (1)

(b) (i) Food poisoning can make a person vomit and have diarrhoea. This makes them lose water. Give **one** important function of water in the body. (1)

(ii) Vomiting can bring acid from the stomach into the mouth. How could this harm the teeth? (1)

(c) It is possible to give a vaccine against some types of bacteria that cause diarrhoea. How does a vaccine help to control infection by bacteria? (2)

7 Material cycles and photosynthesis

1 Which option best completes each of the following sentences?

(a) During photosynthesis a leaf uses _____ (1)

oxygen	starch
carbon dioxide	protein

(b) Root hair cells have a large surface area to _____ (1)

photosynthesise more efficiently

absorb minerals and water

make contact with other roots

store excess carbohydrate

(c) An animal cell does not have _____ (1)

a membrane	cytoplasm
a nucleus	chloroplasts

(d) A plant cell differs from an animal cell because the plant cell
has _____ (1)

a nucleus	cytoplasm
a cell membrane	a cell wall

(e) The energy needed to drive the process of photosynthesis comes
from _____ (1)

conduction from heat in the soil

decomposition of carbohydrates

light from the sun

heat in rainwater

(f) The roots of a plant absorb _____ (1)

water and minerals

water and carbon dioxide

carbon dioxide and minerals

nitrates and light

(g) The most important part of a plant cell for the absorption of light energy is the _____ (1)

cell wall   cell membrane

chloroplast   nucleus

(h) The tissue that transports sugars through the body of a plant is the _____ (1)

xylem   starch

blood   phloem

2   Andy carried out an experiment to investigate whether carbon dioxide is needed for photosynthesis. The experiment was set up as shown in the diagram below:

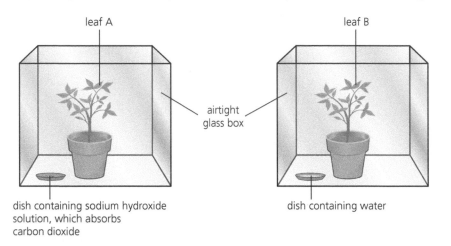

dish containing sodium hydroxide solution, which absorbs carbon dioxide

dish containing water

To find out whether photosynthesis had taken place, Andy tested leaves for the presence of starch. Starch is made from glucose.

(a) (i)   Write out the word equation for the process of photosynthesis.   (2)

   (ii)   Name the chemical that is used to test for starch.   (1)

   (iii) What would be a positive result of such a test?   (1)

(b) Which one of the leaves would you expect to show the presence of starch?   (1)

Explain your answer.   (2)

(c) (i)   What is unusual about leaf C in this diagram?   (1)

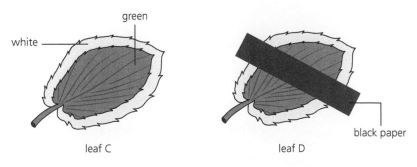

leaf C   leaf D

    (ii)   How would you remove all of the starch from these leaves? (1)

    (iii) Both of these leaves were destarched, then exposed to bright light for 6 hours. Draw a diagram to show what the leaves would look like if they were now tested for starch. (2)

3   Billy bought a potted plant for his grandma's birthday. She tried to look after it, but after a while she noticed that the leaves were turning yellow.

(a) (i)   What is the name of the green pigment in plants? (1)

    (ii) Which mineral is needed for the plant to make this pigment? (1)

    (iii) What does the plant use the pigment for? (1)

(b) A potted plant is more likely to suffer from a mineral shortage than a plant growing in the garden. Explain why. (1)

(c) Billy wanted to buy some houseplant fertiliser for his grandma's plant. His science teacher said that he could mix his own and suggested the following substances.

A — Ammonium nitrate   B — Magnesium sulphate   C — Potassium nitrate   D — Calcium superphosphate

    (i)   Give the letter of one substance he would need to include to make sure that his fertiliser contained each of the following minerals: (2)

- potassium
- phosphate
- nitrate
- magnesium

    (ii)   Sometimes excess fertilisers can be washed into lakes and rivers. If this happens, the oxygen content of the water can fall. This can prevent organisms from carrying out aerobic respiration.

        Give **two** ways in which anaerobic respiration is less useful than aerobic respiration. (2)

    (iii) Some of the leaves fell off grandma's plant and lay on the soil beneath it. They slowly broke down into simpler molecules. Name **one** type of organism that might carry out this breakdown. (1)

4   Which option best completes each of the following sentences?

(a) A process that can raise carbon dioxide levels in the environment is _____ (1)

denitrification   photosynthesis

combustion   leaching

(b) Bacteria and fungi are useful in the environment because they

_____ (1)

work as producers

act as carnivores

break down waste materials

are photosynthesisers

(c) While it is dark, a plant _____ (1)

respires and photosynthesises

respires only, using oxygen

photosynthesises only, using carbon dioxide

respires only, using carbon dioxide

5   Amna used the apparatus shown below to measure how the concentration of carbon dioxide affected the rate of photosynthesis.

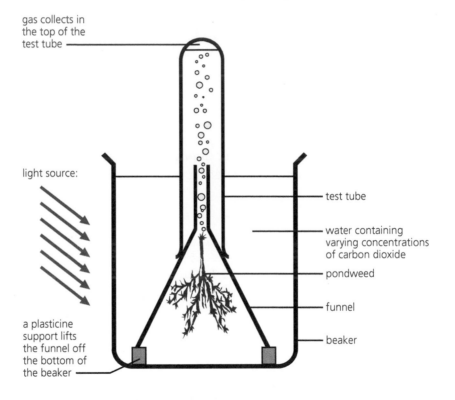

gas collects in the top of the test tube

light source:

a plasticine support lifts the funnel off the bottom of the beaker

test tube

water containing varying concentrations of carbon dioxide

pondweed

funnel

beaker

She obtained the following results:

Concentration of carbon dioxide in %	Rate of photosynthesis in number of bubbles released per minute
0.05	7
0.10	13
0.15	20
0.20	26
0.25	30
0.30	31
0.50	31

(a) (i) Plot the results from the table on the previous page on a grid like the one below. (4)

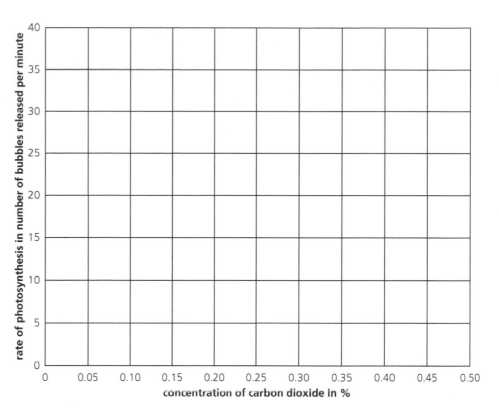

(ii) Use your graph to find at what concentration of carbon dioxide the plant produced 24 bubbles per minute. (1)

(iii) What does the graph tell you about how a greenhouse owner could grow his plants most efficiently? (2)

(b) When Amna carried out this investigation she wanted it to be a fair test. Name **three** factors she should control for this to be true. (3)

(c) Amna thought that the gas given off by the plant was oxygen.

(i) How could she test if this was true? (1)

(ii) Amna's teacher said that the number of bubbles released was not an accurate way of measuring the rate of photosynthesis. How could Amna measure the volume of gas accurately? (1)

(iii) How could Amna make her results more reliable? (1)

6 Hydrogencarbonate indicator solution changes colour according to changes in pH.

pH	Colour of indicator
Neutral or very slightly acidic	Red
Acidic	Yellow
Alkaline	Purple

Five test tubes were set up as shown in the diagram below. Red hydrogencarbonate indicator solution was added to each of the tubes. The tubes were left on a sunny window ledge for 3 hours.

A
contains
small snails

B
contains
pondweed

C
contains small
snails and
pondweed

D
(wrapped in black
paper) contains
pondweed

E
(control)

(a) (i)   Which acidic gas, produced by living organisms, is likely to affect the acidity of the indicator solution? (1)

(ii) After 3 hours what would be the colour of the indicator solution in test tube A? (1)

(iii) Explain your answer. (1)

(b) (i)   What would be the colour of the indicator solution in tube B? (1)

(ii) Explain your answer. (1)

(iii) The colour of the indicator solution did not change in tube C. Explain why. (1)

(c) What was the purpose of the control (tube E)? (1)

8 Relationships in an ecosystem

1 Which option best completes each of the following sentences?

(a) Fungi can _____ (1)

photosynthesise   attack and eat small animals

break down waste materials   replace plants in the environment

(b) Plants increase the biomass in the environment through the process
of _____ (1)

absorption   respiration

seed production   photosynthesis

(c) The flow of energy between living organisms is _____ (1)

an example of respiration   a food chain

a pyramid of numbers   photosynthesis

(d) A chemical used to detect a product of photosynthesis
is _____ (1)

iodine solution   hydrogencarbonate indicator solution

litmus solution   oxygen gas

(e) A simple method of measuring the size of a population uses
a _____ (1)

ruler   measuring cylinder

quadrat   set square

(f) In a simple food chain a predator would be _____ (1)

a herbivore   a fungus

a carnivore   the Sun

(g) The producer in an ecosystem is always a _____ (1)

large animal   fungus

green plant   small animal

2   Copy the words in the boxes below and then draw lines to match up each term with the best description. There are more descriptions than terms.   (4)

Ecological term
Nitrate
Competition
Population
Conservation

Description
All the members of the same species living in one area
Managing the environment for the benefit of wildlife
Needed by plants in the habitat to make chlorophyll
A mineral often added to farmland in fertilisers
Two or more organisms trying to obtain the same thing from their environment

3   The diagram shows a food web in the sea close to Antarctica.

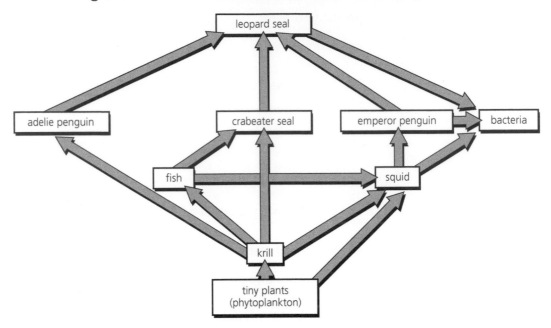

(a) (i)   Identify an example of each of the following   (4)

  • a herbivore

  • a producer

  • a carnivore

  • an organism that breaks down waste materials

(ii)   Draw out a food chain of five organisms selected from this food web.   (2)

(b) Emperor penguins feed on squid. Squid swim very quickly and have a slippery skin.

Suggest **two** ways in which the Emperor penguin is well adapted to catching its prey.

4 Which option best completes each of the following sentences?

(a) The final size of a population is **not** affected by _____ (1)

the method used to count the organisms

competition for food

the number of disease-causing organisms

the number of predators

(b) The top carnivore in a habitat is always _____ (1)

a bird   a fox

very small   an animal

(c) Each of the following is an example of pollution except
for _____ (1)

excess chemicals flowing into rivers

poisonous chemicals being sprayed onto crops

woodland being cut down

sulfur dioxide being released from car engines

(d) A habitat does **not** provide _____ (1)

food   breeding sites

predators   shelter

5 The graph below shows how the population of wild trout in a lake changed over
a period of time.

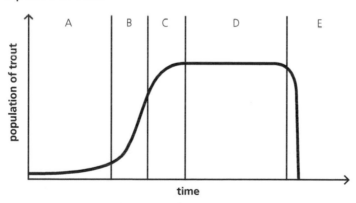

(a) (i) What does the section labelled D tell you about the birth rate and
the death rate of the trout during this time period? (1)

(ii) Explain how you know this. (1)

(b) (i) Which part of the curve shows when the fish began to compete with
each other for food? (1)

(ii) Explain how you know this. (1)

(iii) Suggest **one** other factor that might be affecting the population curve at this point. (1)

(c) A fish farmer decides to grow trout in enormous nets in a Scottish loch. He provides the food for the trout and then catches them for sale.

(i) He wants the trout to grow quickly. Which nutrient should the trout food contain to make sure that this happens? (1)

(ii) The trout food is expensive and the fish farmer wants to make a profit. A population of farmed trout will grow along the same curve as the population of wild trout shown in the graph. Which section of the population curve represents the best time for him to catch the fish for sale? (1)

(iii) Explain your answer. (2)

6 The diagram shows part of a farmland food chain.

lettuce   snail   thrush   hawk

(a) The number of organisms at each stage of the food chain can be represented by a pyramid.

(i) Copy this pyramid and then write the name of each organism alongside the bars of the pyramid. (1)

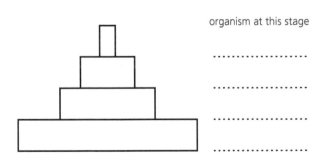

organism at this stage

....

....

....

....

(ii) The thrush has many ticks (small parasites) living under its feathers. Redraw the pyramid of numbers to show this. (2)

(b) The thrushes look for some of their food in gardens and are often killed and eaten by cats. Explain the effect of this on **snails** and **lettuces**. (2)

(c) Farmers are encouraged to leave hedgerows around their fields. Suggest **two** reasons why this might increase the population of thrushes. (2)

7 Deforestation removes many tens of thousands of trees every year.

(a) Nearby farms are often flooded when forests have been cut in this way.
   Explain why.   (1)

(b) Rainforests are important habitats for many animals. Give **two** reasons
   why fewer animals can survive if trees have been removed.   (2)

(c) Fallen leaves and fruits from the cut trees can be decomposed
   (broken down).

   (i)   Which types of organism carry out this breakdown?   (1)

   (ii) During this breakdown heat is released. Which biological process is
         responsible for this release of energy during decomposition? (1)

   (iii) Some of the energy released in the process described in part (ii) appears
         as heat. Some small forest lizards pile up decomposing leaves over
         their eggs. This incubates the eggs until the young lizards hatch out.
         The proportion of male and female lizards that hatches is affected
         by the temperature of incubation. Biologists have collected eggs and
         incubated them at different temperatures. The results are shown in
         the following table.

Temperature in °C	Percentage of lizards hatching as males	Percentage of lizards hatching as females
26	0	100
28	0	100
30	0	100
32	21	79
34	78	22
36	100	0
38	100	0

Plot these results on a grid like the one below. (3)

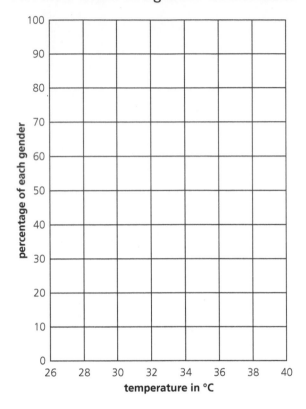

(iv) Conservationists want to release the lizards back into a suitable habitat. They would like to release one male for every female. Why do they need to release males and females in equal numbers? (1)

(v) Use the graph to estimate the temperature at which 50% of the hatching lizards will be male and 50% will be female. (1)

9 Variation, classification, evolution and inheritance

1   Which option best completes each of the following sentences?

(a) Butterflies are insects because they _____ (1)

lay eggs   have three main body parts

can fly   feed on nectar

(b) The genes that control the characteristics of a cell are part of
    the _____ (1)

membrane   cytoplasm

nucleus   chloroplasts

(c) An insect is classified as an arthropod because it _____ (1)

has wings   has jointed limbs

has three main body parts   lays eggs

(d) A child receives genes from both parents at the time of _____ (1)

conception   menstruation

ovulation   fertilisation

(e) Polar bears have thick white fur and live in snowy areas. This is an example
    of _____ (1)

adaptation   variation

development   growth

(f) An eagle is a bird because it _____ (1)

has scales   can fly

has a beak   feeds on other birds

(g) Arranging living things into groups of related organisms is
    called _____ (1)

fertilisation   variation

adaptation   classification

(h) _____ is an example of discontinuous variation. (1)

the mass of different seeds in a seed pod

blood group in humans

height of oak trees

chest circumference in men

(i) A section of DNA that codes for the production of one protein
is a _____ (1)

chromosome   cell

nucleus   gene

2 Use the key to identify the coral reef fish.

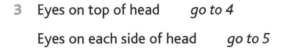

  1 Shape is very long and thin   *go to 2*

     Shape is not long and thin   *go to 3*

  2 Fins are pointed   *trumpetfish*

     Fins are smooth   *eel*

  3 Eyes on top of head   *go to 4*

     Eyes on each side of head   *go to 5*

  4 Has a long, thin tail   *ray*

     Has a blunt tail   *plaice*

  5 Has stripes   *go to 6*

     Does not have stripes   *boxfish*

  6 Has dark tips to fins and tail   *clownfish*

     Does not have dark tips to fins and tail   *angelfish*

3 Sally kept five chickens in her garden.

The table below contains some information about these chickens.

Name of chicken	Sex of chicken	Number of eggs laid per year
Amy	Female	98
Beth	Female	125
Chrissie	Female	105
Dannie	Female	95
Eric	Male	0

(a) Sally wants to increase the number of eggs per year by using selective breeding.

(i)   Which two chickens should she breed together? (1)

(ii) Sally lets some of the eggs hatch and the chickens become mature. She chooses chickens to breed from among these offspring.

Which ones should she choose? (1)

(b) There are other characteristics of the chickens that might be used during selective breeding.

Choose from this list the **two** characteristics that are the **most** useful. (2)

- colour of feathers
- amount of milk produced
- size of eggs
- low life expectancy
- size of beak
- resistance to disease

4   The drawings show mice from two different breeds.

(a) (i)   Give **two** ways in which the mice are different. (2)

(ii) These differences were inherited from their parents. What is the name of the parts of the chromosomes that control these differences? (1)

(iii) Which **two** types of cell pass this information from the parents to their offspring? (2)

- blood cell
- sperm cell
- cell lining an air sac
- skin cell
- egg cell

(b) Freddy thought the colour differences between the mice were due to their diet. He had one pair of mice that had a litter of 16 babies and decided to feed half of them on a diet containing black pigment and the other half on a diet without the pigment. He thought that he would be ready to collect his results after 28 days.

(i) What is the **input** (independent) **variable** in this investigation? (1)

(ii) What is the **outcome** (dependent) **variable** in this investigation? (1)

(iii) Suggest **two** other factors that Freddy should control to make sure that this is a fair test. (2)

(c) After 28 days Freddy observed that the two groups of mice showed no colour differences. He concluded that the differences were due to which of the following? (1)

- genes and environment
- environment only
- genes only
- chance only

5 Living organisms can be classified according to characteristics they have.

(a) Which **three** of the following characteristics are likely to be the most useful for classifying animals? (3)

- the type of skin it has
- how heavy it is
- whether or not it has a bony skeleton
- how fast it can run
- how long it is
- whether or not it has eyes

(b) Copy the words in the boxes below and then draw lines to match the descriptions of living organisms with the name of the classification group. (5)

Group	Description of characteristics
Spider	Cells with a definite cell wall but no chlorophyll
Insect	Produces spores and cells contain chlorophyll
Fungus	Two body parts and eight jointed legs
Fern	Body is made of a single cell, with a clear nucleus and cytoplasm
Protist	Three body parts and six jointed legs

6 Which option best completes each of the following sentences?

(a) Some animals move to new habitats when conditions are harsh. This is an example of _____ (1)

hibernation   conservation

variation   migration

(b) Fungi are not included in the plant kingdom because they do not _____ (1)

reproduce

respire

photosynthesise

excrete

(c) One of the following human characteristics is not affected by environment. It is _____ (1)

body mass

eye colour

height

arm strength

(d) The mass of the individual apples on an apple tree is controlled by _____ (1)

genes only

genes and some effect of the environment

the environment only

the species of tree

7   Samir and Nisar were investigating certain features of other members of their year group at school.

(a) The first feature they investigated was whether each of their friends had 'joined' ear lobes or 'hanging' ear lobes.

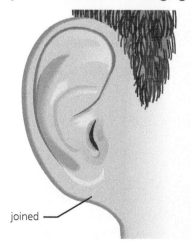
joined

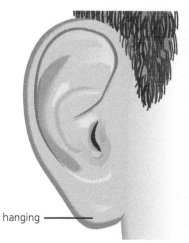
hanging

They recorded their results in a table.

Joined ear lobes	Hanging ear lobes
22	8

Use a chart like the one below to draw on a bar to show how many pupils had 'joined' ear lobes. (2)

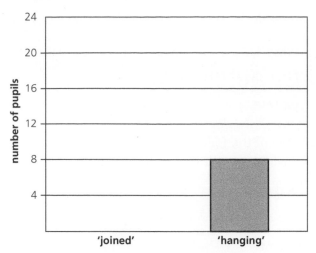

(b) Next they investigated the length of the forearm (from the elbow to the tip of the middle finger).

(i) Why was it important that each pupil kept their arm straight during the measurement? (1)

This bar chart shows their results.

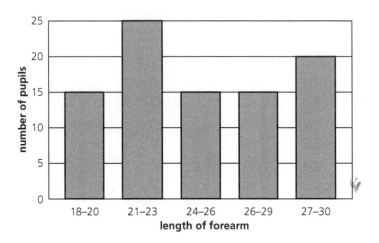

(ii) What units do you think they used for their measurements of forearm length? (1)

(iii) Give **one** mistake in the way they grouped the arm lengths in their bar chart. (1)

(c) Samir and Nisar also checked whether or not the pupils could roll their tongue into a U-shape. They found that the pupils either could do this or they could not. There was nobody who could 'half roll' their tongue, or 'three quarters roll' it. Copy the table below and then use a tick (✔) or a cross (✗) to complete the table. (2)

Characteristic	Inherited only	Inherited and affected by the environment
Shape of ear lobe		
Length of forearm		
Ability to roll tongue		

(d) Nisar said that the features they had investigated depended on the pupils' parents.

  (i) Explain how a child can look like both parents but **not** be identical to either of them. (2)

  (ii) There was one set of identical twins in the year group that they investigated. Why do identical twins have identical characteristics? (1)

8 The diagram below shows five mammals.

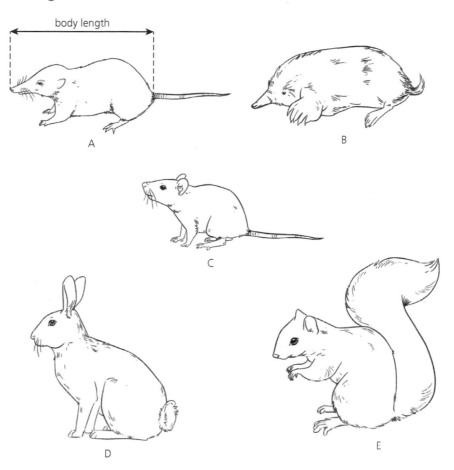

(a) Use the key to identify each of these mammals. Write the letter for each mammal in the table that follows.

  1 Tail more than half body length   *go to 2*

  Tail less than half body length   *go to 4*

  2 Ears on top of head, with thick tail   *Sciurus caroliniensis*

  Ears on side of head, with straight, thin tail   *go to 3*

  3 Nose pointed   *Sorex araneus*

  Nose blunt   *Clethriononomys glareolus*

  4 Front legs wider than long   *Talpa europea*

  Front legs longer than wide   *Oryctolagus cuniculus*

Name of mammal	Letter
Clethriononomys glareolus	
Oryctolagus cuniculus	
Sciurus caroliniensis	
Sorex araneus	
Talpa europea	

(b) This diagram shows a young deer feeding from its mother.

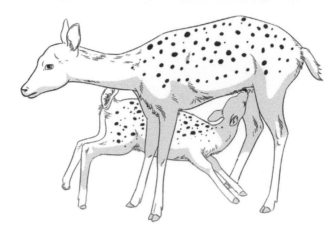

State two features of the deer, visible in this diagram, that distinguish
mammals from other vertebrates. (2)

9 A scientist working in Scotland believed that
otters were so good at catching fish because
they could keep their bodies warmer in cold
water. He used very small data loggers to
record the body temperatures of both fish
and otters in water at different temperatures.
This graph shows his results.

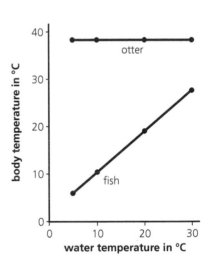

(a) Higher body temperatures speed up the
action of cells involved in respiration and
digestion, and make muscles more flexible.
Explain why the scientist thought that the
otters were at an advantage if the water
was at only 5°C. (3)

(b) The water temperature close to the outflow from a power station rose
to 25°C. What would happen to the body temperature of:

(i)   the otter? (1)

(ii) the fish? (1)

(c) This image shows an otter.

    (i) From the image, give **two** ways in which the otter is adapted for swimming quickly underwater. (2)

    (ii) The otter is a mammal. Give **one** feature, not shown in the image, that is shared by all mammals. (1)

    (iii) The otter will eat frogs, grass snakes and even ducklings. Give **one** feature that is shared by otters, fish, frogs, snakes and ducklings. (1)

(d) The scientist noticed that not all of the fish were the same length, even though they looked the same otherwise. What is this an example of? (1)

CHEMISTRY

 Experiments in chemistry

1 Which option best completes each of the following sentences?

(a) A colourless gas that turns limewater milky is _____ (1)

oxygen   hydrogen

carbon monoxide   carbon dioxide

(b) Anhydrous copper sulfate can be used to test for water. If water is present, anhydrous copper sulfate turns from _____ (1)

blue to white   blue to pink

blue to black   white to blue

(c) A colourless gas that will relight a glowing splint is _____ (1)

oxygen   hydrogen

carbon monoxide   carbon dioxide

(d) The hottest part of a Bunsen flame is _____ (1)

bright yellow   deep blue

pale blue   red-orange

(e) A factor that a student chooses to change during the course of an experiment is _____ (1)

a fixed variable   a controlled variable

an independent variable   a dependent variable

(f) A gas that is released when zinc reacts with hydrochloric acid burns with a 'pop'. The gas is _____ (1)

chlorine   hydrogen

oxygen   carbon dioxide

(g) A piece of apparatus used to measure and transfer small volumes of liquids is _____ (1)

a burette   a measuring cylinder

a pipette   an evaporating dish

2   Jenna and Saed were investigating the heating power of Bunsen burners. They began by checking whether the burner delivered more heat with the air hole open or with it closed. They measured the heat energy from the Bunsen burner by finding out the time taken for some water to boil.

(a) (i)   What is the **input** (independent) **variable** in this experiment? (1)

(ii)   What is the **outcome** (dependent) **variable** in this experiment? (1)

(b) Variables should be controlled to make this a fair test. Which of the following are the **three** most important choices? (3)

- the position of the Bunsen burner below the beaker

- the thermometer that was used

- the volume of water in the beaker

- the science lab in which they were working

- the time of day

- the position of the gas tap (i.e. how much flow of gas)

3   This question involves identification of gases. Use the information provided to copy and complete the table below. Choose from the following gases: (5)

oxygen   carbon dioxide

hydrogen   sulfur dioxide

Effect on limewater	pH with universal indicator	Effect on a burning splint	Gas
None	4	Puts it out	
None	7	Goes 'pop'	
Turns it cloudy	6	Puts it out	
None	7	Burns more brightly	

4   Jane was interested in how people measured time in the past. She made two candles, and drew lines on them.

(a) (i)   What would Jane use to measure the volume of wax she used in making the candles? (1)

candle 1

candle 2

(ii)   What would Jane use to measure the distance between the lines? (1)

(b) Jane's idea was to time how long it took for the candles to burn. She burned candle 1 first, and presented her results in this table.

Section that was burned	Time taken to burn in minutes
P to Q	20
Q to R	20
R to S	
S to T	20

(i) Jane drew a graph of her results. The points are plotted on the graph grid below.

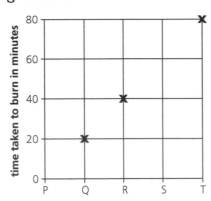

Using a graph like the one above, add the missing value on the graph and join the points. (1)

(ii) Jane then burned candle 2.

Draw another line on your graph, showing roughly how long you think it took for candle 2 to burn between the sections. (1)

(c) Jane thought that the candles could be used to measure time throughout the country. Suggest **three** features of the candles that would have to be kept constant if the candles were going to be reliable timekeepers. (3)

5   Neel used this apparatus to find out which substances are released when ethanol is burned.

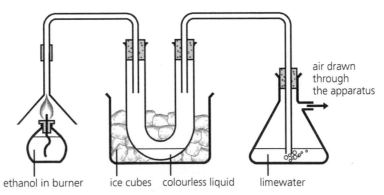

ethanol in burner   ice cubes   colourless liquid   limewater

(a) (i)   Why did he add ice cubes around the U-tube? (1)

(ii)   One of the gases turned the limewater milky. What is the name of this gas? (1)

(iii)   What test should Neel carry out on the colourless liquid in the U-tube? What do you think a positive result would be, and what would the result tell him? (2)

(b) Ethylene glycol is another alcohol, and it is sometimes used in antifreeze. It can be added to the contents of a car radiator to prevent the water freezing as the temperature falls.

ANTIFREEZE
ethylene glycol

percentage antifreeze used (%)	freezing point in °C
10	-5
20	-12
30	-21

(i) There are two hazard warning symbols on the label of the antifreeze container. What **two** precautions would you take if you were using this antifreeze? (2)

(ii) The label on the container also provides information about the effect of the antifreeze on the freezing point of water. Neel had filled his radiator with 2 litres of solution containing 200 cm³ of antifreeze and 1800 cm³ of water. During the night the temperature fell to −18°C. What would happen to Neel's radiator? Explain your answer. (2)

6 (a) Match the following hazard symbols with their descriptions. (Write A =, B = etc.) There are more descriptions than symbols. (5)

A

B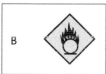

C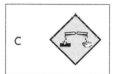

D

E

Oxidising

Highly flammable

Toxic

Harmful

Corrosive

Irritant to eyes or skin

(b) Chemicals can have more than one hazard warning. Which hazards are identified on this petrol container? (3)

PETROL

57

7 Look at these diagrams.

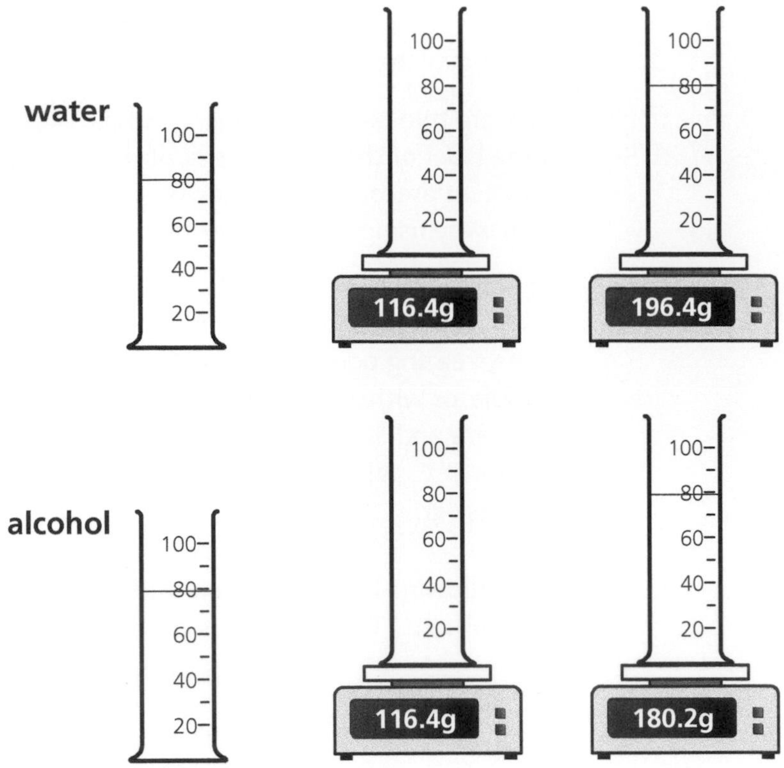

water

100—
80—
60—
40—
20—

100—
80—
60—
40—
20—
116.4g

100—
80—
60—
40—
20—
196.4g

alcohol

100—
80—
60—
40—
20—

100—
80—
60—
40—
20—
116.4g

100—
80—
60—
40—
20—
180.2g

(a) Calculate the density of water and of alcohol. Show your working. (3)

(b) Oil is less dense than water. If a mixture of oil and water is allowed to stand, the oil will float to the top. Name a piece of apparatus that will allow you to remove a small volume of oil. (1)

11 The particulate nature of matter

1   Which option best completes each of the following sentences?

(a) When a solid melts, the particles _____   (1)

vibrate more   vibrate less

vibrate to the same extent   stop vibrating completely

(b) The change of water from liquid to water vapour is _____   (1)

boiling   freezing

evaporation   condensation

(c) During the water cycle, the change of water vapour to droplets of liquid water is _____   (1)

evaporation   condensation

precipitation   boiling

(d) In an experiment to investigate the effect of temperature on evaporation, temperature is _____   (1)

a fixed variable   the control

the outcome variable   the input variable

(e) Particles move through liquids and gases by _____   (1)

concentration   diffusion

dilution   dispersal

(f) Density can be defined as _____   (1)

mass × volume

$\dfrac{mass}{volume}$

$\dfrac{volume}{mass}$

$\dfrac{mass^2}{volume}$

(g) The temperature at which a liquid changes to a gas
is the _____ (1)

    freezing point   condensation point

    boiling point   sublimation point

(h) During a change of state, the mass of a substance _____ (1)

    remains the same

    rises

    falls

    may or may not change depending on the two states involved

2 Sulfur is an element that can exist as a solid, a liquid or a gas. The diagram
below shows sulfur in different states, and the letters A, B, C and D represent
changes of state between solid, liquid and gas.

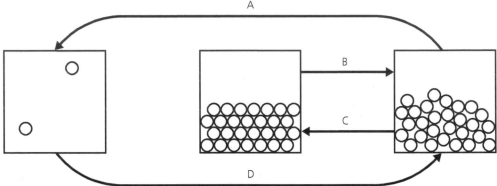

(a) What is change of state A called? (1)

(b) What is change of state B called? (1)

(c) What is change of state C called? (1)

(d) What is change of state D called? (1)

3 Which option best completes each of the following sentences?

(a) Salty water _____ (1)

    freezes at 0°C   above 0°C

    doesn't freeze   freezes below 0°C

(b) Adding impurities to water causes its boiling point to _____ (1)

    lower   rise

    stay the same   rise to twice its original level

4   The volume of an object can be found by the displacement of water, and its mass can be found using a weighing machine. Juno wanted to find out if her brooch was made of silver and so made the following measurements.

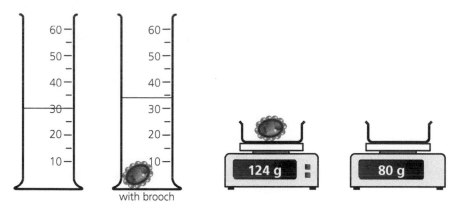

with brooch

(a) Calculate the volume of the brooch. Show your working.   (2)

(b) Calculate the mass of the brooch. Show your working.   (1)

(c) Calculate the density of the brooch. Show your working.   (2)

(d) Silver has a density of 10.2 g per cm³, lead has a density of 11.5 g per cm³ and nickel has a density of 8.9 g per cm³. Is the brooch silver?   (1)

5   The diagram below shows the water cycle.

(a) Add labels to the diagram to show where evaporation, condensation and rainfall take place.   (3)

(b) The diagram below shows the state of water in different stages of the water cycle and the arrangement of particles.

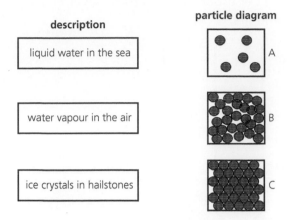

description   particle diagram

| liquid water in the sea | A |

| water vapour in the air | B |

| ice crystals in hailstones | C |

Draw lines to match the descriptions of water's state with the particle diagrams. (3)

6   All the pupils in the class decided to celebrate their teacher's retirement. They bought a lot of rubber party balloons and filled half with helium and the other half with air. They then wrapped the balloons in coloured aluminium foil. Each balloon contained exactly the same volume of gas.

(a) Explain why the air-filled balloons drop to the ground but the helium-filled balloons rise. (2)

(b) The diagram below shows a number of arrangements of particles.

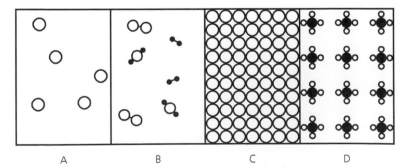

A   B   C   D

Which letter represents:

(i)   the helium gas? (1)

(ii) the aluminium foil? (1)

(c) Over a period of a week the balloons shrink because the particles of gas escape. The helium-filled balloons shrink more quickly.

    (i)   Name the process by which the particles of gas move.   (1)

    (ii) Why does helium escape more quickly than air from a balloon?   (1)

7   The diagram shows a can of pressurised propane, used as a fuel for burning paint from wooden window frames. Most of the propane in the can is in the liquid state, but some of it is gas.

    (a) (i)   What happens to the pressure inside the can when the temperature falls? Explain your answer.   (2)

       (ii)   What would happen to the flame from the paint burner if the painter were using it out of doors on a cold day?   (1)

       (iii) There is a warning on the can not to throw it into a fire. Why is this important?   (1)

    (b) Which of these statements about the propane liquid in the can are correct?   (3)

    The molecules of the liquid are:

- smaller than
- the same distance apart as
- closer together than
- moving faster than
- the same size as
- bigger than
- further apart than
- moving more slowly than

    } those in the gas

8   Some solid wax was slowly warmed in a boiling tube. The temperature of the wax during the warming process was measured using a temperature sensor connected to a data logger.

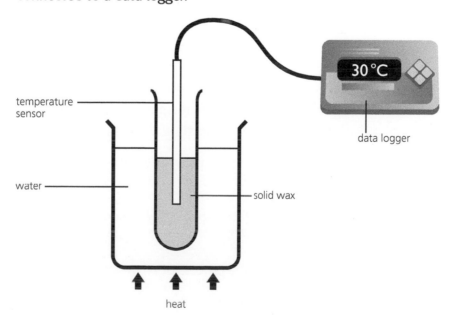

    temperature sensor

    30 °C

    data logger

    water

    solid wax

    heat

A graph of the results looked like this:

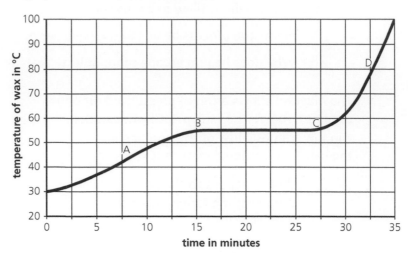

(a) (i) At what point on the graph (A, B, C or D) did the wax begin
to change state? (1)

(ii) Explain your answer. (2)

(iii) What is the physical state of the wax at point D? (1)

(b) Suggest **two** advantages of carrying out the investigation using a
temperature sensor and data logger rather than a thermometer. (2)

(c) This particular wax boils at 275°C. Why can the wax not boil during
this investigation? (1)

(d) Describe and explain the differences between the movement of the
water molecules at the start and the end of the investigation. (2)

9 Robert Brown observed pollen grain particles moving around on the surface of
cold water. This is called Brownian motion.

A teacher set up a model to show Brownian motion. It is shown in the diagram
below. The ping-pong balls will not roll off the speaker because it has a raised edge.

(a) The teacher turned on the power supply. The loudspeaker started to vibrate.
Predict what will happen to the ping-pong balls and small balloon. (1)

(b) State what the ping-pong balls and small balloon represent in this model
of Robert Brown's observations. (2)

(c) Use the model to explain why the pollen grain particles that Brown
observed moved. (3)

(d) Suggest how the process of Brownian motion can be used to explain
diffusion. (2)

12 Atoms, elements and compounds

1 Which option best completes each of the following sentences?

(a) A typical metal _____ (1)

    is not a good conductor of electricity

    does not have a high melting point

    is not usually dull in appearance

    is not malleable

(b) A substance made of only one type of atom is _____ (1)

    pure   an element

    likely to be of low density   an alloy

(c) The particles in a liquid are likely to be _____ (1)

    in a regular fixed pattern   not moving

    moving slightly   far apart

(d) Copper reacts with oxygen to produce _____ (1)

    a gas   an oxide

    an acid   an element

(e) An element that can conduct electricity is _____ (1)

    oxygen   iron

    sulfur   nitrogen

(f) The simplest particles found in matter are _____ (1)

    molecules   compounds

    atoms   elements

(g) The particles in a compound are called _____ (1)

    atoms   elements

    molecules   reactants

(h) The chemical symbol for iron is _____ (1)

    I   Fe

    Ii   In

(i) The number of elements in sulfuric acid, H_2SO_4 is _____ (1)

1	6
3	8

(j) the approximate proportion of oxygen in air is _____ (1)

0.03%	21%
6%	79%

2   The drawings show different elements that have been used to produce different objects.

(a) Copy the words in the boxes below and then draw lines to match the element to the reason for using it. (5)

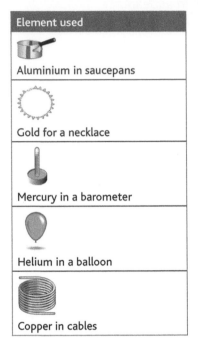

Element used	Reason for choosing this element
Aluminium in saucepans	It is lighter than air
Gold for a necklace	It is a good conductor of heat
Mercury in a barometer	It conducts electricity and is easy to stretch
Helium in a balloon	It stays shiny because it does not react with oxygen in air
Copper in cables	It stays liquid at room temperature

(b) Elements can have more than one property.

(i) Name **two** properties of copper that would make it suitable for use in the solid base of expensive saucepans. (2)

(ii) Name a property of helium that makes it suitable for storage in metal cylinders. (1)

3   Scientists were collecting material from the bottom of the Pacific Ocean. One of them believed that he had found a new metallic element – he called it oceanium.

(a) Which **two** properties suggest that oceanium could be a metal? (2)

- It glows in the dark.

- It is a green solid.

- It has a high melting point.

- It is a good conductor of heat and electricity.

- It does not stick to a magnet.

(b) One of the scientists tried adding some dilute acid to the solid. The result was a blue solution with green solids floating in it.

Name **one** method he could use to separate the floating green solids from the solution.

4 This list shows a number of properties of different materials.

A   non conductor of electricity

B   poor conductor of heat

C   magnetic

D   can be compressed

E   good conductor of heat

F   very flexible

G   very high melting point

H   good conductor of electricity

Match the properties with the statements below by selecting letters to fill the blanks. (5)

(a) _____ : makes plastic a good material for the handle of a kettle.

(b) _____ : makes it possible to pump a lot of air into a bicycle tyre.

(c) _____ : makes cotton a good material for shoelaces.

(d) _____ and _____ : **two** properties that make aluminium a good material for cooking pans.

5 A group of pupils carried out a class practical in which they burned magnesium in air. They wished to record the mass of magnesium used and any change in the mass as burning took place.

(a) Draw and label a set of apparatus they might use to carry out this investigation. (3)

(b) The results are shown in the table below.

Pupil	Mass of magnesium in g	Mass of product in g
Jack	6.4	10.4
Sam	3.8	6.5
Neela	4.8	8.4
Anja	6.1	10.7
James	2.7	4.0
Billy	4.2	7.0

(i) What is the name of the product that is formed? (1)

(ii) Present the results from the table above on a grid like the one below. Draw a line of best fit. (4)

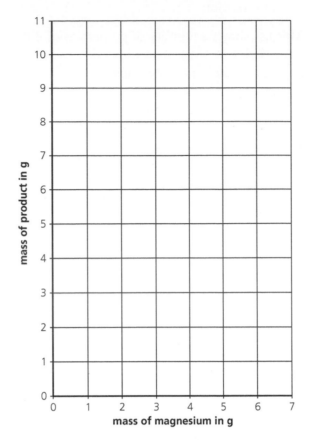

mass of product in g

mass of magnesium in g

(iii) Use the graph to predict the mass of magnesium required to provide 7.5 g of product. (1)

(iv) Use the graph to predict how much product will be formed if 5.5 g of magnesium is burned in air. (1)

(v) Give one conclusion you can draw about the relationship between the mass of magnesium burned and the mass of product formed. (2)

6 John Dalton used symbols like the ones shown here to represent atoms.

Some possible combinations of these atoms are shown in these diagrams.

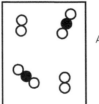 A

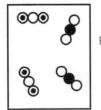 B

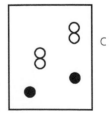 C

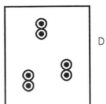 D

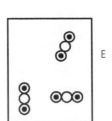 E

(a) (i) Give the letter that shows a mixture of an element and a compound. (1)

(ii) Give the letter that shows only a compound. (1)

(b) Give **one** difference between a compound and a mixture. (1)

(c) (i) Suggest a name and formula for the substance represented in D. (1)

(ii) Suggest names and formulae for the substances represented in C. (2)

7 The table shows the melting points and boiling points of some elements.

Element	Melting point in °C	Boiling point in °C
Sodium	98	883
Mercury	−39	357
Iron	1538	2861
Oxygen	−219	−183
Gold	1064	2856

(a) Which element is liquid at room temperature (approximately 21°C)? (1)

(b) Which element is a non-metal? (1)

(c) Magnesium chloride is formed when magnesium and chlorine combine together in a chemical reaction. Write the symbols for magnesium and chlorine. (2)

(d) The formula for a substance is FeS. What is the name of this substance? (1)

(e) Calcium burns brightly in oxygen, forming calcium oxide (CaO). Calcium oxide reacts with water, forming a compound with the formula $Ca(OH)_2$.

(i) Name the compound with the formula $Ca(OH)_2$. (1)

(ii) This compound is slightly soluble in water. Predict the colour of universal indicator when mixed with the solution. (1)

13 Mixtures, separation and solubility

1 Which option best completes each of the following sentences?

(a) Pure water is _____ (1)

a solution	a mixture
a compound	an element

(b) A mixture made of a solvent and an insoluble substance can be _____ (1)

a solution	an oil
a suspension	a solute

(c) The change of state from liquid to gas is _____ (1)

condensation	distillation
melting	evaporation

(d) A separation method that separates a solid from a liquid by careful pouring is _____ (1)

distillation	decanting
filtration	evaporation

(e) An example of a mixture is _____ (1)

iron filings	water
air	sodium chloride

(f) A pure substance _____ (1)

contains particles of only one type

contains only atoms

contains different elements arranged in different ways

cannot form part of a mixture

(g) _____ is **not** true for the gas carbon dioxide. (1)

it forms about 0.03% of the atmosphere

it is a product of photosynthesis

it is produced when energy is released in aerobic respiration

it is a compound

(h) _____ is **not** true for the gas oxygen. (1)

it is needed for combustion to take place

it is needed for aerobic respiration

it is produced during photosynthesis

it is a compound

(i) The Liebig condenser is a piece of apparatus used for separation of _____ (1)

a solvent from a solution   several different soluble substances

a solid from a liquid   gases from the air

(j) The change of state from vapour to liquid is _____ (1)

condensation   distillation

melting   evaporation

2   The following are different ways of separating the components of mixtures:

A   simple distillation

B   with a magnet

C   chromatography

D   filtration

Choose one of the letters to show which is the best method to obtain:

(a) iron from a mixture of iron filings and sulfur (1)

(b) water from seawater (1)

(c) chalk from a mixture of chalk and water (1)

(d) food colourings from sweets (1)

3   Jack had a leaking ballpoint pen, which left a stain on his trouser pocket.

His science teacher rubbed some ethanol on to the stain with a tissue, and noticed that the tissue developed a purple stain and the stain on his trousers became lighter.

(a) Explain how the ethanol helped to remove the stain. (2)

(b) The teacher asked Jack whether he thought that the ballpoint ink was made of one type of dye or several.

(i) Name the technique that Jack could use to find out. (1)

(ii) Jack obtained the following results:

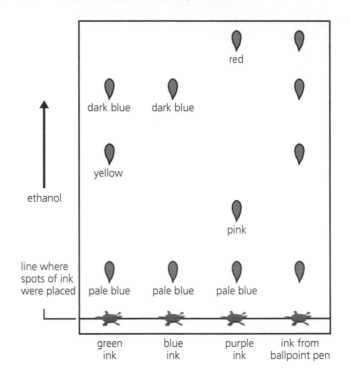

Which colours were present in the ballpoint ink? (1)

(iii) How many coloured substances were there in the blue ink? How do you know? (1)

(iv) Which word is the best one to describe each coloured substance? (1)

- solution

- solvent

- solute

- suspension

4   Sara and David were investigating the effect of solute concentration on the boiling point of water. They measured out different masses of salt and dissolved each sample in a different 500 cm³ of water. They then measured and recorded the temperature at which the water boiled.

(a) (i) What is the **independent (input) variable** in their investigation? (1)

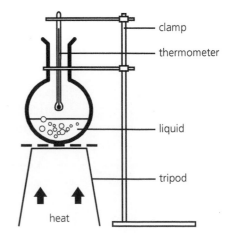

(ii) What is the **dependent** (outcome) **variable** in their investigation? (1)

(iii) They had a list of possible **fixed** (controlled) **variables**. From this list choose **two** that must be controlled, and **one** that would have little or no effect on their results. (3)

- volume of water
- type of salt dissolved in water
- starting temperature of water
- room temperature

(b) They wrote down their results in this table.

Mass of salt added in g	Boiling point in °C
0	100
10	100.6
20	103
30	104
40	106
50	result lost
60	109.2

(i) Plot their results on a grid like the one below. (3)

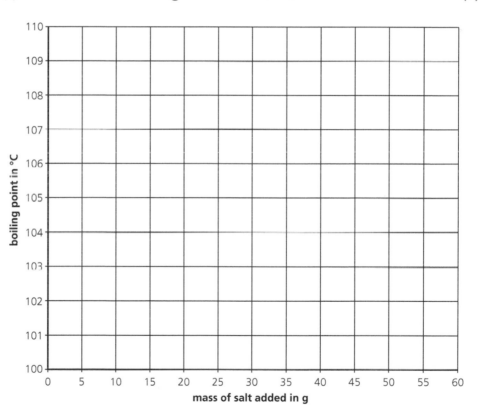

(ii) From your graph, suggest a likely result for the one, at 50 g of salt added, which they lost. (1)

(iii) Predict the temperature at which a solution of 100 g of salt in 500 cm³ of water would boil. Show your working. (2)

heat

5 Sally added some copper sulfate crystals to a beaker of water.

(a) (i) How could she see that some of the crystals had dissolved in
the water? (1)

(ii) What could she do to increase the amount of the copper sulfate
that dissolved? (1)

(b) How could Sally collect copper sulfate crystals from the
solution in the beaker? (1)

(c) Sally carried out an experiment to investigate how much of three food
flavourings will dissolve in water at different temperatures. The results are
shown in the graph below.

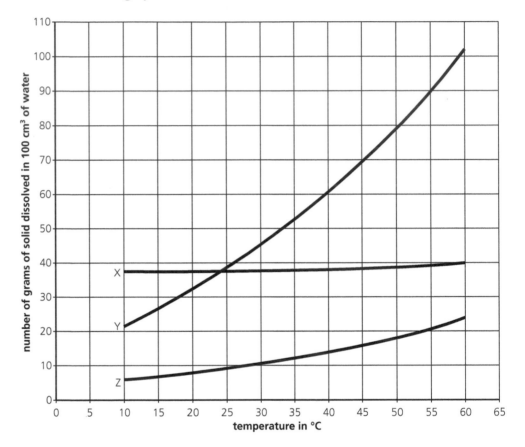

(i) How many grams of flavouring Z dissolved in the water at 40°C? (1)

(ii) Which flavouring dissolved best at 20°C? (1)

(iii) Which **two** flavourings are equally soluble at 24°C? (1)

6 Abi added some sugar to 100 cm³ of cold water in a beaker. She stirred the water
to dissolve the sugar, and then added more sugar until no more would dissolve.

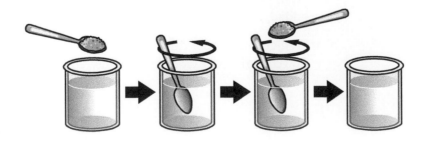

She repeated the experiment with salt, curry powder and instant coffee. Each time, she used a different beaker containing 100 cm³ of cold water. The results are shown in the bar chart below.

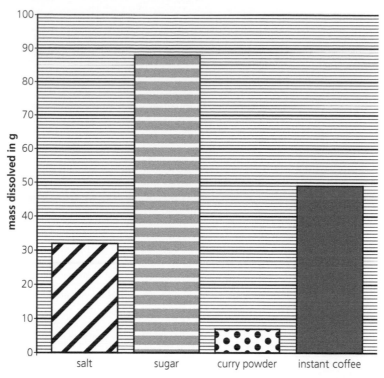

(a) (i) State **two** ways in which Abi made this a fair test. (2)

(ii) Which substance was the least soluble in water? (1)

(iii) How many times more soluble was sugar than salt? Give your answer to 1 decimal place, and show your working. (3)

(b) When Abi makes a cup of coffee for her father, the coffee dissolves much more quickly. Explain why. (1)

7 A science teacher set up the apparatus shown, with a solution of a water-soluble food dye in the flask.

(a) (i) What is the name of the separation process which the teacher is demonstrating? (1)

(ii) During the demonstration, which pair of processes will occur? (1)

- melting then evaporation

- condensation then evaporation

- melting then boiling

- evaporation then condensation

(b) The teacher says that the liquid that is collected in the beaker is pure water. Describe **one** test that would show the liquid is **water** and another test that would show that it is **pure** water. (2)

(c) (i) Water at 20°C enters the condenser at X. Predict the temperature of the water when it leaves the condenser at Y. (1)

(ii) Explain your answer. (1)

(iii) Give **two** ways in which the water vapour is changed as it passes down the glass tube in the condenser. (2)

8 Copy the words in the boxes below and then draw lines to match the terms with their correct definitions. (3)

Term	Definition
Concentrated	A mixture of a solvent and a solute
Saturated	The liquid part of a solution
Solution	A solution with many solute particles in a small volume of solvent
Solvent	The amount of a substance that will dissolve in a liquid
Solubility	Able to dissolve
Soluble	A solution that cannot accept any more solute

 **Chemical reactions**

1 Which option best completes each of the following sentences?

  (a) Each of the following is a sign that a chemical reaction has taken
     place except for _____ (1)

     heat being released   a new substance being formed

     the reaction being reversible   fizzing often occurring as a gas
                                       is formed

  (b) The products of fermentation do not include _____ (1)

     carbon dioxide   glucose

     heat   ethanol

  (c) If a hydrocarbon is burned in air, the products are _____ (1)

     carbon dioxide + water   carbon + water

     carbon dioxide + carbon monoxide   carbon monoxide + water

  (d) Hydrochloric acid and magnesium oxide react together to produce
     magnesium chloride and water. This type of reaction is an
     example of _____ (1)

     reduction   neutralisation

     oxidation   recombination

  (e) Each of the following is a fossil fuel except for _____ (1)

     natural gas   coal

     oil   wood

  (f) Spoilage of food is an example of a harmful chemical reaction.
     Food cannot be preserved by _____ (1)

     adding extra water   drying

     removing oxygen   keeping food in acidic conditions

  (g) _____ is **not** a chemical reaction. (1)

     photosynthesis   separation of a mixture of iron filings
                             and sulfur

     respiration   burning natural gas in air

2 Copy the boxes below and then draw lines to match the chemical
   reactions with their possible uses. (4)

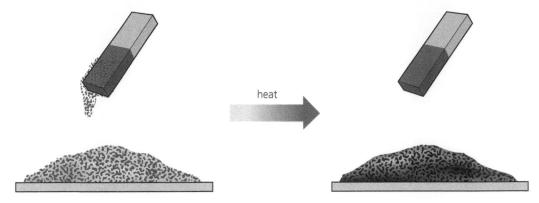

Reaction	Use for the reaction
iron oxide + carbon monoxide → carbon dioxide + iron	For plants to make food
methane + oxygen → carbon dioxide + water	To extract a metal from its ore
water + carbon dioxide → glucose + oxygen	To release energy in living organisms
glucose + oxygen → carbon dioxide + water	To transform chemical energy to thermal energy for heating

3 A science teacher heated iron filings and sulfur on a tray.

heat

(a) (i)   Write out a word equation for this reaction. (1)

    (ii) From the information in the diagram give **one** piece of evidence
          that a chemical reaction has occurred. (1)

(b) (i)   Suggest the name and the formula for the solid formed when
          zinc is heated with sulfur. (2)

    (ii) Some fossil fuels contain sulfur. When fossil fuels burn, sulfur
          reacts with oxygen. Write out a word equation for this reaction. (1)

    (iii) What **type** of chemical reaction is this? (1)

4 This apparatus can be used to burn
   magnesium ribbon in air. The process was
   demonstrated by a science teacher.

   (a) (i)   Explain why the teacher told
             the pupils that they should
             never look directly at burning
             magnesium. (1)

       (ii) The teacher wanted to make a note
             of the changes in mass during the
             reaction. He told the pupils that
             he was going to gently rub the
             magnesium ribbon with a piece of
             abrasive paper before beginning the
             experiment. Why was this important? (1)

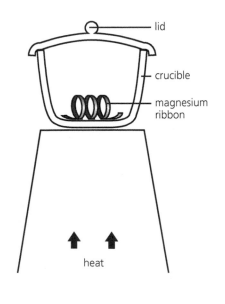

lid

crucible

magnesium
ribbon

heat

(b) The following results were obtained:

Mass of crucible in g	50	50	50	
Mass of crucible + magnesium ribbon in g	63	61	62	
Mass of crucible + contents after heating in g	69.8	70.1	70.1	

(i) Copy and complete the table by writing in the mean values for the measurements in the shaded column. (1)

(ii) Explain these results. (2)

(iii) Write out a word equation for the reaction that has taken place during the demonstration. (1)

5 Which option best completes each of the following sentences?

(a) A substance that will not decompose on heating is _____ (1)

copper sulfate   calcium carbonate

copper   copper carbonate

(b) When potassium permanganate is heated, oxygen is given off.

This is an example of _____ (1)

oxidation   sublimation

decomposition   combustion

(c) A chemical reaction between a metal and the air that takes place without burning is _____ (1)

decomposition   combustion

reduction   corrosion

(d) A metal that is higher in the reactivity series than a second metal will **not** _____ (1)

react faster with water than the second metal

burn more vigorously in air than the second metal

be displaced from its oxide by the second metal

react faster with dilute acids than the second metal

(e) The equation that represents fermentation (anaerobic respiration in yeast) is _____ (1)

sugar → lactic acid + energy

sugar → alcohol + carbon dioxide + energy

alcohol + carbon dioxide → sugar + energy

sugar → alcohol + energy

6   The table below contains some information about the sources and effects of greenhouse gases.

Name of gas	Sources of gas	Percentage overall contribution to the greenhouse effect
Methane		14
CFCs	Aerosols, refrigerants and coolants	21
	Burning forests and fossil fuels, manufacture of cement	
Nitrogen oxides	Breakdown of fertilisers, burning fuel in internal combustion engines	7
Low-level ozone	Combination of nitrogen oxides with oxygen	2

The only other greenhouse gas is water vapour, which contributes 2% to the greenhouse effect.

(a) Copy and complete the table, by writing into the shaded boxes the source of methane, the main greenhouse gas and the percentage contribution it makes to the greenhouse effect. (2)

(b) Suggest three possible harmful results of the greenhouse effect. (3)

(c) Burning fossil fuels also causes air pollution, including acid rain. Lakes that have been acidified by acid rain have very little remaining aquatic life. Some lakes have been treated by adding large quantities of calcium hydroxide, which quickly dissolves in the lake water.

   (i)   What effect will this have on the pH of the lake? (1)

   (ii) When the calcium hydroxide reacts with the sulfuric acid in the lake, a salt is formed. What is the name of this salt? (1)

   (iii) Write a word equation for the reaction which produces this salt. (1)

7   Plants need nitrogen to grow well. Farmers add nitrogen-containing fertilisers to soil to increase crop yield. The fertilisers are manufactured chemically.

   (a) (i)   Complete this equation for the production of fertiliser. (2)

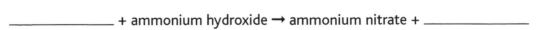

   _____ + ammonium hydroxide → ammonium nitrate + _____

   (ii) What type of chemical reaction is this? (1)

   (b) Scientists in an agricultural laboratory investigated how the mass of ammonium hydroxide decreased during this reaction. They presented their results in the form of a graph.

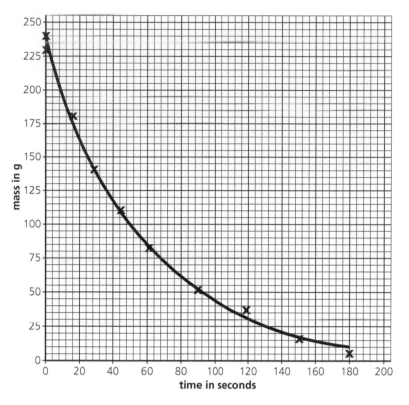

(i) Over which 30 s period did the mass of ammonium hydroxide decrease most quickly? (1)

(ii) The mass of ammonium hydroxide was 240 g at the start. How long did it take for the mass to decrease by 75%? Show your working. (2)

8 A manufacturer of model figures was interested in changing the material used to cast the models.

The manufacturer mixed two components of the resin, and then left the resin to swell. The resin needs to swell before it can be poured – it only hardens when it is baked above 200°C. This diagram shows the changes in volume of the resin over a 30-minute period.

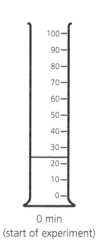
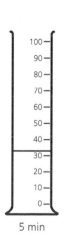
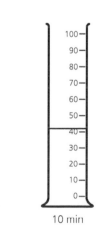
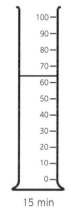
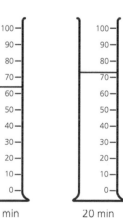
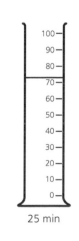
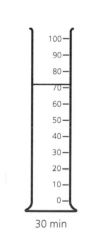

0 min
(start of experiment)
5 min
10 min
15 min
20 min
25 min
30 min

(a) (i) Copy and complete the table below, using the manufacturer's results. (2)

Time in minutes	Volume of resin mix in cm³
0	
5	
10	
15	
20	
25	
30	

(ii) Draw a line graph of these results on a graph grid like the one below. (3)

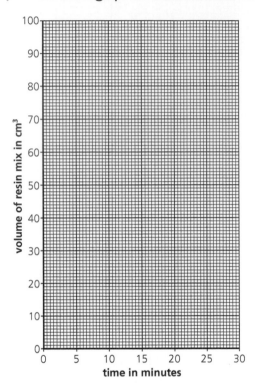

(iii) The manufacturer believed that he would get the most stable resin if he only allowed the mix to swell to two and a half times its original size. Use the graph to predict how long he would need to leave the mix to achieve this result. (1)

(b) He decided to add different quantities of a hardener to see the effect on the volume of the resin mix.

(i) What is the **input** (independent) **variable** in this investigation? (1)

(ii) What is the **outcome** (dependent) **variable** in this investigation? (1)

(iii) Give **two** other variables which the manufacturer would need to control if this were to be a fair test. (2)

(c) One feature of the hardened resin is that it does not react with air or with water. Suggest why this is important in the finished models. (1)

9 Two factors affect the heat delivered by a Bunsen burner – the supply of gas from the gas tap and the supply of air through the air hole.

(a) The hottest Bunsen flame is achieved when _____ (1)

the gas tap is fully on and the air hole closed

the gas tap is fully on and the air hole half open

the gas tap is half on and the air hole half open

gas tap is fully on and the air hole fully open

(b) The hottest part of the Bunsen burner flame is _____. (1)

the cone of the flame   the blue part of the flame

inside the barrel   just behind the open air hole

10 A student placed an iron nail inside a 25 cm³ measuring cylinder. He added boiled water until the meniscus reached the 15 cm³ mark, then sealed the measuring cylinder. Within a few days the nail began to show signs of rust, and the water level began to rise.

(a) Explain why the water level began to rise. (1)

(b) Explain why boiled water was used in this experiment. (1)

After a long period the nail was very rusty and the water level stopped rising.

(c) Predict the level to which the water had now risen. (1)

(d) Explain your prediction (1)

The student carefully removed the nail from the water.

(e) The nail would be _____ (1)

heavier than at the start of the experiment

lighter than at the start of the experiment

the same weight as at the start of the experiment

(f) Explain your answer to (e). (1)

11 The following paragraph is about damage to stone buildings. Copy and complete it by filling in the missing words, chosen from this list. (5)

acid rain   combustion   granite   limestone
nitrogen   sulfur dioxide   sulfuric acid

_____ of fossil fuels produces the gas _____. This gas dissolves in water in the atmosphere to produce _____, which falls as _____. This compound can cause damage to buildings, especially those formed from _____.

15 The reactions of metals

1 Which option best completes each of the following sentences?

(a) When iron is added to lead chloride solution, lead metal is formed. This type of reaction is a _____ (1)

neutralisation	displacement
decomposition	combustion

(b) Reduction is when an oxide reacts and loses its oxygen. When iron is heated with copper oxide, the mixture glows and copper and iron oxide are formed. In this reaction _____ (1)

both copper and iron are oxidised

iron is oxidised and copper is reduced

both copper and iron are reduced

copper oxide is decomposed

(c) A metal that is unreactive and so would be suitable for electrical contacts is _____ (1)

iron	magnesium
aluminium	silver

(d) When copper carbonate is heated, the reaction that takes place is _____ (1)

neutralisation	displacement
decomposition	combustion

(e) When copper is heated strongly in an open dish its mass will _____ (1)

increase	decrease
stay the same	increase then decrease

(f) the chemical symbol for sodium is _____ (1)

So	Na
S	Su

(g) _____ is **not** a property of metals. (1)

often shiny	good conductors of heat
malleable	low density

(h) The following elements all conduct electricity, but _____ is **not** a metal. (1)

iron   copper

graphite   nickel

(I) Metal railings can rust, so they must be made of _____ (1)

aluminium   lead

copper   iron

(j) _____ must be present for metal railings to rust. (1)

carbon dioxide and oxygen   water and carbon dioxide

oxygen and water   water and hydrogen

2   Jack was investigating the reaction between metals and hydrochloric acid. He added 20 cm³ of hydrochloric acid to each of five test tubes, then placed equal-sized pieces of metal into four of the tubes.

iron	zinc	magnesium	copper	
+	+	+	+	
hydrochloric acid	hydrochloric acid	hydrochloric acid	hydrochloric acid	hydrochloric acid

(a) (i)   What was the **independent** (input) **variable** in this investigation?   (1)

(ii)   What was the **dependent** (outcome) **variable** in this investigation?   (1)

(iii)   How was the outcome variable measured?   (1)

(iv)   Name **two** steps that Jack took to ensure that this was a fair test.   (2)

(b) Arrange the four metals in order of their reactivity, with the most reactive first.   (1)

(c) Jack wanted to know where gold would fit into this series, but his teacher said that gold was too expensive.

(i)   Predict the result that Jack would have obtained if he **had** been allowed to use it in his investigation.   (1)

(ii)   Explain your answer.   (1)

3 Ahmed was concerned that his bike was rusting, so tried to work out the conditions for rusting. He set up five test tubes containing iron nails, as shown below.

    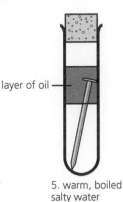

layer of oil

1. water + air   2. salty water + air   3. warm water + air   4. warm salty water + air   5. warm, boiled salty water

He presented his results as a bar chart, shown below.

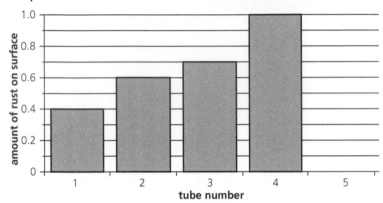

(a) (i) Copy the bar chart and add the missing bar for tube 5.   (1)

Give a reason for the size of the bar.   (1)

(ii) Which had the bigger effect on rusting – salt or warmth?   (1)

Give a reason for your answer.   (1)

(b) Ahmed set up a sixth test tube: this one contained a nail in vinegar. He saw that the iron nail reacted with the vinegar.

(i) Is vinegar acidic, alkaline or neutral?   (1)

(ii) During the reaction, bubbles of gas were given off.
What was this gas?   (1)

(iii) If the gas could be collected, how could you test your answer?   (1)

(c) Zinc is sometimes used to galvanise metal surfaces and prevent rusting.

(i) How does zinc prevent rusting?   (2)

(ii) Why is galvanising not used on bicycle chains?   (1)

4 Jane added some magnesium to copper sulfate solution. She noticed that the blue solution turned paler and that the solution became warm.

(a) (i) What is this sort of reaction called?   (1)

(ii) Copy and complete the equation for this reaction.   (2)

magnesium + copper sulfate → _____ + _____

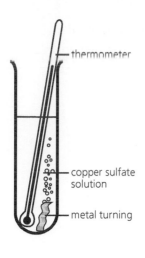

thermometer

copper sulfate
solution

metal turning

(b) Jane decided to investigate the rise in temperature as the reaction proceeded. She repeated her experiment with magnesium, and also tried zinc and iron. She used the apparatus shown here.

Her results are shown in the table below.

Metal added to copper sulfate solution	Starting temperature in °C	Final temperature in °C	Rise in temperature in °C
Magnesium	21.5	84.0	
Zinc	22.0	39.5	
Iron	23.0	34.5	

(i) Copy and complete the table by calculating the rise in temperature for each of the metals added. (1)

(ii) Part of the reactivity series is shown below. Copy this and add magnesium and copper in the correct positions. (1)

- sodium

- calcium

- _____

- aluminium

- zinc

- iron

- lead

- _____

Use this reactivity series to explain:

(iii) why there was little difference in the results obtained for zinc and iron (1)

(iv) whether there would be a rise in temperature for any of the following mixtures:

- calcium and zinc sulfate (1)

- lead and zinc chloride (1)

- aluminium and sodium chloride (1)

5 In the extraction of iron from iron ore, haematite (iron oxide) is reacted at high temperature with coke (carbon) in the presence of oxygen. The oxygen combines with the carbon to form carbon monoxide.

(a) Copy and complete this word equation for the reaction between carbon monoxide and iron oxide. (3)

_____ + _____ → _____ + carbon dioxide

(b) The cast iron produced in this way is brittle, and is usually modified in some way to make it more useful. The table below shows the percentage of carbon in four different materials.

Material	Percentage of carbon
Cast iron	4.0
Wrought iron	0.2
High-carbon steel	0.8
Mild steel	0.4

(i) High-carbon steel is used for some knife blades. What proportion of the carbon must be removed from cast iron to produce high-carbon steel? Show your working. (2)

(ii) The highest-quality knife blades are made from stainless steel. This is made by removing most of the carbon and adding small amounts of other metals. What is the main advantage of stainless steel? (1)

(c) The graph below shows how the percentage of carbon affects the strength of the materials in the table: the strength is measured using a very complex type of force meter.

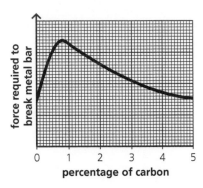

(i) What is the percentage of carbon in the material with the greatest strength? (1)

(ii) Which is the strongest material in the table in (b)? (1)

6 (a) Copper is best described as:

- an element

- a compound

- a metal

- a metallic element (1)

(b) Metals are usually found as compounds, and must be extracted from these compounds before they can be used.

(i) What is the name given to these naturally occurring metal compounds? (1)

(ii) Which one of these metals is most usually found in its 'free' state (i.e. not in a compound)? (1)

iron   copper

silver   aluminium

(c) An iron nail is placed into some silver nitrate solution. A reaction takes place between the iron and the silver nitrate.

  (i) Copy and complete this word equation for the reaction. (3)

  iron + _____ → _____ + _____

  (ii) Copy and complete the table below to predict whether or not a reaction will take place when each of the metals is added to the named solutions. You may use the reactivity table in question 4 to help you. (4)

Place a ✔ to show that a reaction takes place and a ✗ if no reaction occurs.

Salt solution	Metal			
	Copper	Iron	Magnesium	Zinc
Iron nitrate				
Zinc nitrate				
Calcium nitrate				

(d) Gold does not tarnish (go dull), but aluminium often does. Explain why. (1)

 **Acids, bases and indicators**

1 Which option best completes each of the following?

(a) A substance that can attack other materials, including human
skin, is _____ (1)

    basic   corrosive

    strong   an indicator

(b) A substance that gives up hydrogen in a chemical reaction
is _____ (1)

    a base   an acid

    a metal   an alkali

(c) A chemical reaction between an alkali or base and an
acid is _____ (1)

    neutralisation   oxidation

    indication   decomposition

(d) A solution with a pH of 7 is _____ (1)

    acidic   basic

    corrosive   neutral

(e) One product of a neutralisation reaction is _____ (1)

    an acid   an alkali

    a salt   an indicator

(f) A compound that reacts with an acid to release carbon
dioxide is _____ (1)

    a base   a carbonate

    carbon monoxide   a metal chloride

(g) A gas that turns limewater milky is _____ (1)

    hydrogen   nitrogen

    oxygen   carbon dioxide

(h) Acids react with metals to produce _____ (1)

    salt + water   salt + hydrogen

    water vapour   salt + carbon dioxide

(i) An alkali will always turn _____ (1)

    litmus paper red   universal indicator yellow

    litmus paper blue   limewater milky

(j) The chemical formula NaOH represents _____ (1)

    nitrogen hydroxide   sodium hydroxide

    sodium chloride   sodium hydride

2 The pH of a soil sample can be tested by shaking the soil with water, letting the particles settle and then adding universal indicator solution.

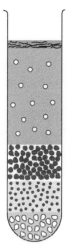

This table shows the pH values of six soil samples.

Sample	pH value
A	8.0
B	7.5
C	7.0
D	8.0
E	4.5
F	6.0

(a) Which soil sample would give a green colour with the universal indicator solution? (1)

(b) Cauliflower and sprouts grow better in alkaline soil. In which soil samples should cauliflower and sprouts grow well? (1)

(c) Rhododendron is a shrub which grows better in acidic soils. In which of the soil samples would the rhododendron grow well? (1)

(d) Crushed and heated limestone can be dissolved in water to produce calcium hydroxide. This calcium hydroxide (slaked lime) is sometimes added to acidic soils. Name the type of reaction that takes place between the lime and the soil. (1)

3   Hydrochloric acid is an example of a strong acid, and is produced in the stomach during the digestion of food.

(a) A student added five drops of hydrochloric acid to a small volume of universal indicator solution in a test tube.

   (i) What colour is the mixture of indicator and hydrochloric acid likely to be? (1)

   (ii) Suggest a likely value for the pH of the hydrochloric acid. (1)

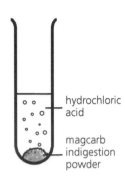

hydrochloric acid

magcarb indigestion powder

(b) Too much hydrochloric acid produced in the stomach can be a cause of indigestion. Magcarb indigestion tablets contain magnesium carbonate, and can be crushed into a powder. If the powder is added to hydrochloric acid in a test tube the mixture will fizz.

   (i) Copy and complete the word equation for the reaction which is occurring. (2)

hydrochloric acid + _____ → _____ + _____ + water

   (ii) Use this equation to explain why the mixture fizzed after addition of the powdered tablets. (1)

   (iii) The student continued to add powder to the acid, and noticed that the mixture stopped fizzing. Why did the fizzing stop? (1)

(c) Which of the following words could be used to describe magnesium carbonate? (2)

a solvent   an element

a salt   an indicator

a mixture   a compound

4   Wasps and bees are both insects that defend themselves using stings. The 'sting' involves the injection of a solution through the skin. The pH values of the 'stings' are shown below.

■ Bee sting, pH 2

■ Wasp sting, pH 10

(a) Copy and complete the table below to show whether the stings are acid or alkaline, and suggest what colour they would change universal indicator solution to. (4)

	Acid or alkaline	Colour of indicator solution
Wasp sting		
Bee sting		

(b) Some common household substances can be used to neutralise wasp and bee stings. Six of these substances are shown in the table below.

Substance	pH value
Water	7
Washing soda	11
Baking soda	8
Bicarbonate toothpaste	8
Vinegar	5
Lemon juice	3

Give the name of one substance in the table that could neutralise:

(i) a wasp sting (1)

(ii) a bee sting (1)

(c) Why is it useful that toothpaste is slightly alkaline? (2)

(d) Nettle leaves contain small cells that release formic acid.

(i) Suggest why dock leaves can be used to get rid of the irritation from a nettle sting. (1)

(ii) Why do you think that the relief from the sting is quicker if the dock leaf is crushed up before it is used in this way? (1)

5 Scientists believe that acid rain is caused by gases in the atmosphere. An investigation into the formation of acid rain was carried out by collecting a number of gases. Each of the gases was bubbled through a sample of green, neutral universal indicator solution.

(a) Three of the gases caused the indicator to change colour. Once all the gas samples had been bubbled through the indicator, alkali was added, from a syringe, until the universal indicator changed back to green.

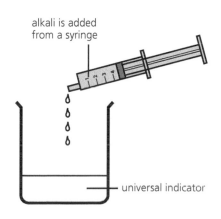
alkali is added from a syringe

universal indicator

The results are shown in the table below.

Gas collected	Change in colour of indicator	Volume of alkali needed to return indicator to green colour incm³
Air	No change	0
Carbon dioxide from burning coal	Green to red	6.9
Exhaust gases from an idling car	Green to red	1.2
Methane from a refuse tip	No change	0
Human breath	Green to yellow	0.2

(i) Which gases formed neutral solutions? (2)

Explain your answer. (1)

(ii) Which gas produced the most acidic solution? (1)

Explain your answer. (1)

(iii) What is the name given to a reaction between an acid and an alkali? (1)

(b) (i) Some metals used in buildings may react with acids in the air. Copy and complete this word equation for this reaction. (2)

copper + carbonic acid → _____ + _____

(ii) Bronze statues often change to a green colour after many years of exposure to the air. Use this word equation to explain why. (2)

6 Jack placed a conical flask on a pan balance. The flask weighed 100 g. He added 50 g of dilute hydrochloric acid and 5.0 g of calcium carbonate to the flask. The total mass of the flask and its contents was 155 g.

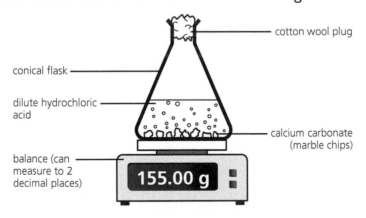

cotton wool plug

conical flask

dilute hydrochloric acid

calcium carbonate (marble chips)

balance (can measure to 2 decimal places)

155.00 g

(a) The calcium carbonate and the hydrochloric acid quickly reacted together. Copy and complete the word equation for the reaction which took place. (3)

calcium carbonate + hydrochloric acid → _____ +

_____ + _____

(b) When the reaction stopped, the total mass had decreased from 155.00 g to 152.70 g. Some water had evaporated from the beaker. What other reason is there for the mass to fall in this way? (1)

(c) How did Jack know that the reaction had stopped? (1)

(d) At the end of the reaction, the calcium carbonate had neutralised the acid. Jack tested a few drops from the flask with universal indicator paper. What is the colour of the universal indicator paper after this test? (1)

(e) Calcium carbonate is a very common compound. Which of the materials in this list are mainly calcium carbonate? (3)

marble	chalk
limestone	coal
sand	glass
glass	

(f) Metals also react with acids.

    (i)   Which gas is produced when a metal reacts with an acid? (1)

    (ii) How would you test for this gas? (1)

7 Sodium hydrogencarbonate (often called bicarbonate of soda) is present in baking powder.

(a) Which of these properties of sodium hydrogencarbonate are especially important for its use as baking powder? (2)

it is very soluble in water	it does not have a smell
it is not poisonous	it is a white solid

(b) Baking powder also contains citric acid. When the baking powder is added to water, the acid and the hydrogencarbonate react together. Explain how this helps to give a light texture to cakes. (1)

PHYSICS

17 Energy sources and transformations

1 Which option best completes each of the following sentences?

(a) Electrical energy can be converted into heat energy by _____ (1)

   a microphone   an LED
   (an iron)   a battery

(b) A bullet fired horizontally from a gun has been given
    mainly _____   (1)
    (kinetic energy)   thermal energy
    sound energy   chemical energy

(c) A unit used to measure energy could be a _____   (1)
    newton   degree
    amp   (joule)

(d) A renewable energy source that depends on naturally occurring
    valleys in mountainous regions is _____   (1)
    wind   solar
    (hydro)   wave

(e) The energy possessed by a rollercoaster car waiting at the top of
    the ride is _____   (1)
    kinetic   (gravitational potential)
    electrical   thermal

(f) An example of a renewable energy source is _____   (1)
    a battery   oil
    (biomass)   coal

(g) A stretched spring stores energy as _____   (1)
    gravitational energy   (strain energy)
    thermal energy   light energy

(h) _____ is the energy source that depends least on the Sun. (1)
    biomass   hydro
    (wind)   tidal

(i) Which of the following is not a fossil fuel?
    (biomass)   natural gas
    oil   coal

2 (a) Copy the words in the boxes below and then draw lines to match the fossil fuels to their common uses. (4)

Fossil fuels
Coal
Natural gas
Petrol
Kerosene

Common uses
Aircraft fuel
Generating electricity in power stations
Heating and cooking in homes
Fuel for cars

(b) Fossil fuels are often described as '**non-renewable**'. What does this mean? (1)

(c) (i) Much of the world's population uses biomass as a fuel. What is biomass fuel? (1)

(ii) Fossil fuels and biomass are both energy resources. What is the original source of this energy? (1)

(iii) Give **one** advantage of using fossil fuel rather than biomass as an energy resource.

3 An explorer has a wind-up torch. This torch is powered by a steel spring, and does not use batteries.

(a) The explorer winds up the spring, and as the spring unwinds, energy is transferred to a small generator. The generator then turns to provide light for the bulb in the torch.

Copy and complete these sentences to describe these energy transfers. (3)

As the spring unwinds it releases stored _____ energy to turn the generator. The movement of the generator produces _____ energy, and in the bulb this is converted to _____ energy.

winder

ECO-TORCH

(b) When the explorer turns the brightness control she notices that the spring unwinds more quickly. Explain why this happens. (1)

4 Which option best completes each of the following sentences?

(a) The spreading of energy from its source is called _____ (1)

diffusion   elimination

translation   dissipation

(b) An electric drill is an example of a machine. When a drill is used there is **no** transformation of electrical energy into _____ (1)

light energy   sound energy

thermal energy   kinetic energy

(c) The law of conservation of energy states that _____ (1)

energy cannot be created or destroyed but can be changed from one form to another

energy input can never exceed energy output for a machine

a machine is never 100% efficient

energy released from a fuel can be changed to many other forms

5   The table below lists six methods of providing energy.

Method	How it works
Log stove	Burns dried wood to provide heat
Wave turbine	Uses wave energy to produce electrical energy
Coal fire	Burns coal to release heat
Solar panel	Uses light energy to provide heat
Petrol generator	Burns petrol to provide electrical energy
Gas boiler	Burns gas to provide heat

(a) (i)   What is the source of energy for a solar panel?   (1)

(ii) Explain how this same source of energy can drive a wind turbine.   (2)

(iii) The forms of energy used in solar panels and wave turbines do not run out as they are used. What are these sources of energy described as?   (1)

(b) Name **two** fossil fuels listed in the table.   (2)

(c) Copy and complete these sentences.   (4)

Biomass fuels (e.g. _____) are made because plants can carry out _____ which converts light energy into stored _____ energy.

A _____ is a device that can use one form of energy to perform some work. When this occurs some energy is always lost as _____.

6   (a) This diagram shows how much heat is lost from different parts of a house.

energy loss = 10 000 J per minute

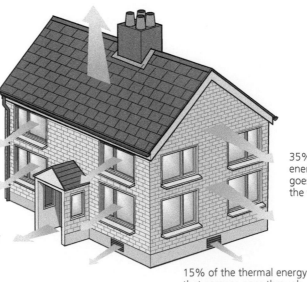

25% of the thermal energy that escapes goes through the roof.

10% of the thermal energy that escapes goes through the windows.

35% of the thermal energy that escapes goes through the walls.

15% of the thermal energy that escapes goes in draughts.

15% of the thermal energy that escapes goes through the floor.

(i) Through which part of the house is most heat lost? (1)

(ii) Cavity wall insulation can reduce heat loss through walls by **75%**. If this house had the walls insulated in this way, what would be the total loss per minute from the insulated house? Show your working. (3)

(iii) Copy and complete these sentences. (3)

Foam injected into the space between walls saves heat energy because the foam is a poor _____ of heat. Loft insulation works in a similar way, because the _____ trapped between strands of fibreglass does not allow heat to escape. Carpets stop heat escaping though the floor, and also help to insulate against _____ transfer.

(b) The diagram shows a simple draught excluder.

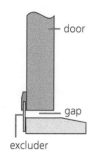

door

gap

excluder

Explain how a draught excluder can help to save heat energy. (2)

7 (a) Some people are worried that if they eat too much fat they will become overweight. Humans use fat obtained from food as a long-term store of energy. The energy content of a fatty food can be investigated using the apparatus shown below:

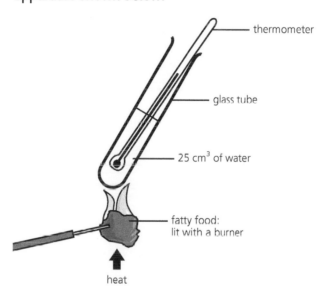

thermometer

glass tube

25 cm³ of water

fatty food: lit with a burner

heat

(i) What is the **input** (independent) **variable** in this experiment? (1)

(ii) What is the **outcome** (dependent) **variable**? (1)

(iii) Give **two** factors that should be kept constant to keep this a fair test. (2)

(iv) 4.2 J of energy will raise the temperature of 1 cm³ of water by 1°C. 1 g of fat contains 38 500 J of energy. Calculate the rise in temperature of 25 cm³ of water if 0.2 g of fat is burned in this way. Show your working and give your answer to the nearest whole number. (3)

(v) In the actual experiment the temperature rise was much less than expected. The science teacher suggested that this might be due to heat losses. Give **two** ways in which heat might be lost and so not heat up the water. (2)

8 Wave (tidal) energy can be used to generate electricity. One possible method is shown in this diagram.

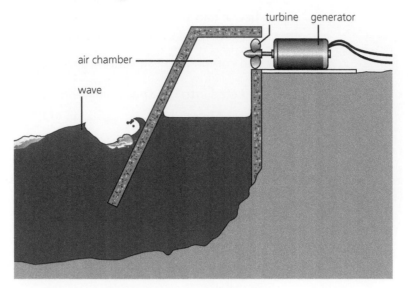

(a) Each box below shows a stage in generating electricity.

A	The turbine turns the generator
B	The moving air turns the blades of the turbine
C	The generator produces electrical energy
D	The waves move up the chamber
E	Air is pushed up the chamber by the waves

What is the correct order?   (2)

(b) A group of engineers investigated how the output of energy from the wave generator depended on the speed of the waves. The results are shown in the table below.

Wave speed in metres per second	0	5	10	15	20	25	30
Energy output in kJ	0	0	7	25	50	78	105

(i) Plot these data on a grid like the one below.   (4)

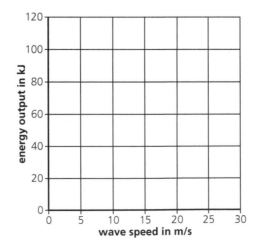

(ii) Suggest why there is no energy output if the wave speed is 5 m/s or less.   (1)

18 Energy and electricity

1 Which option best completes each of the following sentences?

(a) In a power station a jet of steam is used to turn the blades
in a _____   (1)

    furnace   turbine

    boiler   generator

(b) A mobile source of electricity is a _____   (1)

    generator   conductor

    battery   plug

(c) An example of a material that is not a good electrical insulator
is _____   (1)

    glass   plastic

    wood   graphite

(d) Electrical energy can be converted into light energy by
a _____   (1)

    solar panel   battery

    TV monitor   food mixer

(e) Kinetic energy is turned into electrical energy in a _____   (1)

    battery   generator

    petrol engine   bicycle tyre

(f) Chemical energy is turned into electrical energy in a _____   (1)

    wind turbine   generator

    battery   microphone

(g) A lamp turns electrical energy into _____   (1)

    chemical energy and light energy   thermal energy and light energy

    sound energy and thermal energy   chemical energy and thermal energy

(h) A unit used to measure energy could be a _____   (1)

    newton   degree

    amp   joule

(i) A microphone transforms _____ (1)

light energy to sound   sound to gravitational potential energy

sound to light energy   sound to electrical energy

2   Electricity is a very useful form of energy.

   (a) Give **two advantages** and **two disadvantages** of electricity as
       an energy source. (2)

   (b) (i) The diagram below shows a simple electrical circuit. Explain how the
            apparatus could be used to compare the efficiency of **four** different
            materials as insulators. (2)

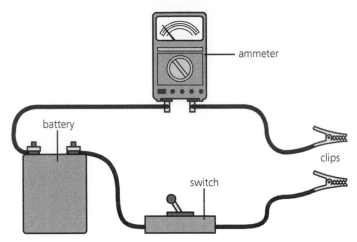

   (ii) Explain **one** way in which you could make sure that this is a fair test. (1)

   (iii) Name **one material** that would be a good insulator, and describe
         one important use of this material. (2)

3   The diagram shows solar panels
    attached to the body of a satellite.

    (a) Scientists measured the output
        from one of these panels during
        one 24-hour period. Their results
        are shown in this diagram:

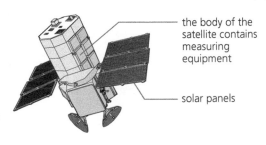

the body of the
satellite contains
measuring
equipment

solar panels

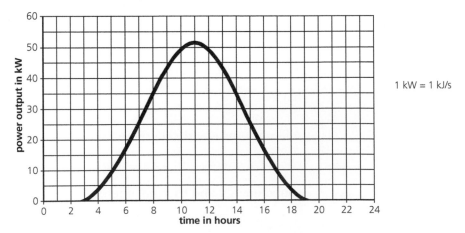

1 kW = 1 kJ/s

   (i) Explain why the power output varied during the 24-hour period. (2)

(ii) The satellite used the solar panel to drive a motor. The motor needs 35 kW to run at full speed. Use the graph to work out how long the motor would be able to run at full speed. (1)

(iii) The scientists decided to improve the design so that the solar panel turns to always face the Sun. Copy the graph and draw another curve to show how the power output for the new, improved solar panel would vary during the 24-hour period. (2)

(b) Why are solar panels so useful on satellites and space stations? (1)

4 The diagram below shows the operation of a power station.

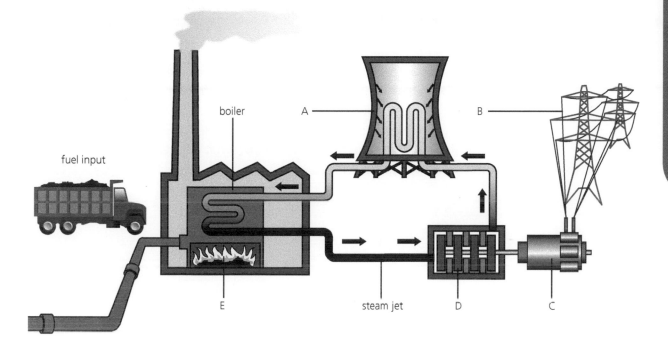

(a) Choose words to complete the labels (A–E) on the diagram – not all of the words need to be used, and some could be used more than once. (5)

furnace   water flow

generator   turbine

solar panel   light for power station

cooling tower   electricity output

(b) The efficiency of a power station describes how much energy is released from a certain mass of fuel. Efficiency is measured in units of gigajoules per tonne.

(i) The table below compares different types of power station. Work out the efficiency of each type of power station, giving your answers to the nearest whole number. (4)

Type of fuel used	Fuel input in (tonnes)	Energy output in gigajoules	Efficiency in gigajoules per tonne
Coal	1000	39 000	
Oil	2000	72 000	
Gas	1500	76 000	
Nuclear	500	21 000	

(ii) Give **two** reasons why we would like to use less coal in power stations. (2)

(iii) Wind power is an alternative to the fuel types in the table above. Give **one advantage** and **one disadvantage** of wind power. (2)

5 A classic car might use a dynamo as a generator. As the engine runs it uses a pulley to turn the generator. The lights on the car are directly connected to the dynamo.

(a) Copy and complete the following sentences. (5)

As the engine runs, _____ energy in the petrol is changed into _____ in the dynamo and this energy is used to provide _____ energy carried in the wires to the lamps. The energy in the wires is changed to useful _____ energy in the bulbs, although some is wasted as _____.

(b) More modern cars would have a battery between the dynamo and the lights. Explain why this is a better arrangement for the car driver. (2)

6 An electrical appliance changes electrical energy into another form that is useful to us. The diagrams below show what happens to the energy supplied to four appliances.

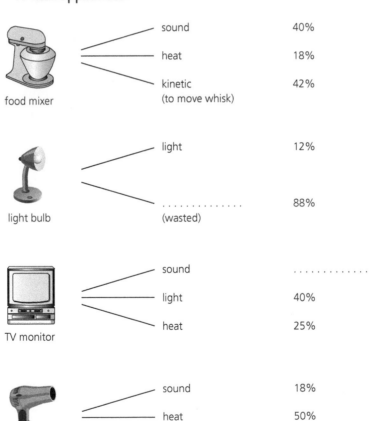

food mixer

sound	40%
heat	18%
kinetic (to move whisk)	42%

light bulb

| light | 12% |
| . . . . (wasted) | 88% |

TV monitor

sound	. . . .
light	40%
heat	25%

hair dryer

sound	18%
heat	50%
kinetic	32%

(a) (i) What percentage of the energy is wasted by the food mixer? (1)

(ii) What percentage of the energy is given out as sound by the TV? (1)

(iii) Much of the energy given out by the light bulb is wasted. What sort of energy is it wasted as? (1)

(b) Two pupils were interested in saving energy in school, and decided to investigate whether all energy-saving light bulbs were equally efficient. They obtained 5 different light bulbs, all rated as 9 watts, and they set up their apparatus as shown in the diagram below.

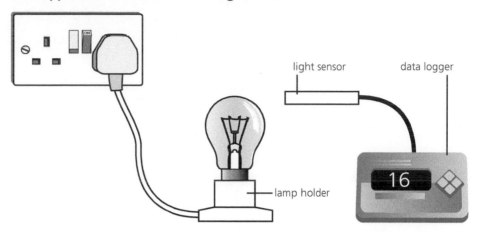

Each bulb was allowed to warm up for the same length of time, and the light sensor was always kept the same distance from the bulb. They repeated each reading three times, and checked each other's readings on the data logger. They obtained the following results:

Brand of bulb	Reading 1	Reading 2	Reading 3	Mean reading
Lumo	16	18	18	
Glo-bright	16	16	16	
Eco-save	18	19	17	
Brite-lite	21	19	20	
Supa-glow	18	18	19	

(i) Calculate the mean value for each bulb. (1)

(ii) Plot these results as a bar chart on a grid like the one shown here. (3)

(iii) Name the **input** (independent) **variable** in their investigation. (1)

(iv) Name the **outcome** (dependent) **variable** in their investigation. (1)

(v) Name **three fixed** (controlled) **variables** that helped to make this investigation a fair test. (3)

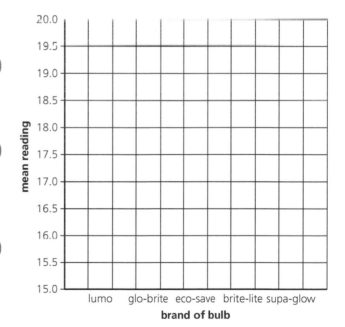

(vi) Explain how the pupils made sure their results were reliable. (1)

(vii) Give **one** conclusion that the pupils could have drawn from their investigation. (1)

19 Forces and linear motion

1 Which option best completes each of the following sentences?

   (a) Two cars are travelling in the same direction on a motorway. The one in the middle lane is travelling at 80 km/h and the one in the outside lane at 94 km/h. Their relative speed is _____ (1)

   $\dfrac{80}{94}$ km/h   −14 km/h

   14 km/h $\dfrac{94}{80}$ km/h

   (b) Speed can be calculated from the formula _____ (1)

   speed = time × distance   speed = $\dfrac{distance}{time}$

   speed = $\dfrac{time}{distance}$ speed = $\dfrac{distance}{time^2}$

   (c) The unit in which force is measured is the _____ (1)

   joule   watt

   kilogram   newton

   (d) A motorcycle is being driven by a force of 100 N. The wind resistance is 28 N. The resultant force moving the motorcycle is _____ (1)

   $\dfrac{100}{28}$ N   −72 N

   $\dfrac{28}{100}$ N   72 N

   (e) Forces always have:

   size only   a size and a direction

   direction only   no value when an object is not moving

2 A drag racing car was being tested over a distance of 500 m. The digital stopwatch used to measure the time taken can measure to 0.01 of a second. The car was tested six times – three times in each direction.

powerful engine

light alloy wheels

(a) The results of the timing are shown in the table below.

Run number	Time taken in seconds
1	6.02
2	6.23
3	6.00
4	6.19
5	8.24
6	6.21

    (i)   Which run was an anomalous result? (1)

    (ii) If the anomalous result is ignored, calculate the mean value for the time taken for the run. Show your working. (1)

    (iii) How does a mean value make the results more reliable? (1)

(b) (i)   What is the formula used to calculate the speed of the car? (1)

    (ii) Calculate the average speed of the car. Show your working, and give your answer to one decimal place. (2)

(c) Give **one** possible reason why the results for runs 2, 4 and 6 were higher than those for runs 1 and 3, other than that the car travelled faster in one direction. (1)

3   The diagram shows a submarine moving on the surface of the sea.

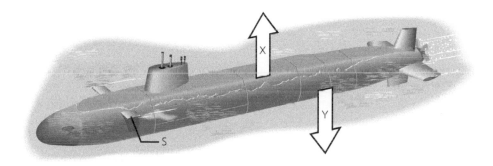

(a) Two of the forces acting on the submarine are marked X and Y. Identify these forces. (2)

(b) The submarine now starts to move away from the dock. Name the **two** forces that resist the movement of the submarine when it is moving quickly. (2)

(c) The commander of the submarine now decides that the vessel should dive below the surface. To do this he must alter the angle of the stabilisers labelled S. Draw a sketch of the submarine and mark on the angle of the stabiliser as the submarine dives beneath the surface. (1)

4 During the school cross-country race, the time taken by one of the boys was measured at different distances around the course. The results are shown in the graph below.

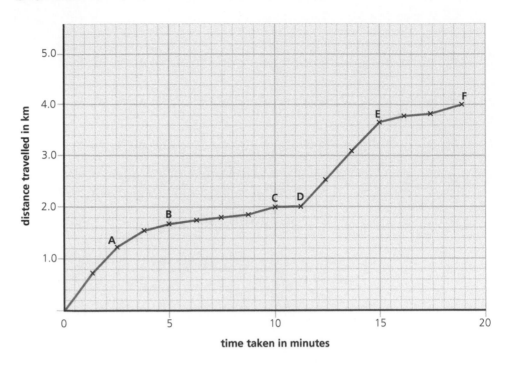

(a) (i) How long did the runner take to complete the course? (1)

(ii) At which point did the boy need to stop and tie his shoelace? (1)

(iii) Which part of the graph suggests that he was running up a steep hill? (1)

(iv) What was the average speed in km per hour over the whole journey? Give your answer to 1 decimal place. Show your working. (2)

(b) (i) Why did the boy wear trainers with ridges and spikes in the soles? (1)

(ii) Copy and complete the following sentence. (3)

During the race, the boy's muscles converted _____

energy into _____ energy (and also into _____

energy, which made him sweat).

5 Which option best completes each of the following sentences?

(a) A metal which has a density of 4 g per cm³ and a mass of 30 g will have a volume of _____ (1)

    10.0 cm³   30.0 cm³

    15.0 cm³   7.5 cm³

(b) The speed of a moving object will remain the same if _____ (1)

it is in a vacuum

all forces on it are balanced

there is no gravity acting on it

there is a constant force on it

(c) Hooke's law applies to _____ (1)

change in speed of an object as a force is applied

extension of a spring as a force is applied

a change in density of a floating object

the calculation of speed

6 Mark Marquez is a champion motorcyclist. His team works on his motorcycle to improve its performance by adding the fairing.

(a) (i) How does the fairing help to improve the speed of the motorcycle? (1)

(ii) The motorcycle does not slide off at the bends because of a force between the tyres and the track surface. What is the name of this force? (1)

(iii) If the motorcyclist falls from the machine it is important that he slides along the track and slowly comes to a halt. What important property of his leather suit helps this? (1)

(b) Mark Marquez's engineers measured the distance travelled by his motorcycle along part of the straight. They obtained these results:

Time in seconds	Distance travelled in m
0	0
1	200
2	399
3	599
4	801
5	1000
6	1201
7	1400
8	1600

(i) Plot these results on a grid like the one below. (3)

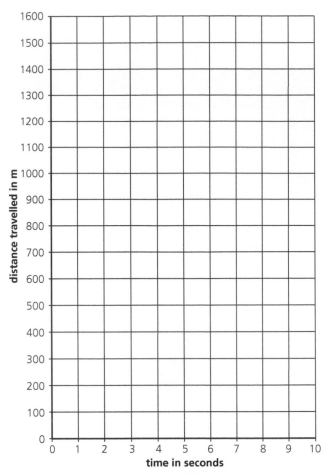

(ii) What was the average speed, in metres per second, during this period? (1)

(iii) From the graph, how far had the motorcycle travelled after 3.5 s? (1)

(iv) How far did the motorcycle travel between 4.5 s and 7.5 s? (1)

(v) If the motorcycle continues at this speed, how long would it take to cover 2.5 km? (1)

7 Karen wanted to investigate the relationship between mass and weight. She used a forcemeter to do this and obtained the following results:

Mass in g	Weight in N
100	1.0
200	2.0
300	3.0
400	4.4
550	5.5
660	6.6

(a) (i) One of the results does not seem to fit the pattern of the other results. Which is the anomalous result? (1)

(ii) Use the information in this table to predict:

- the mass of an object weighing 4.3 N
- the weight of an object of mass 240 g (2)

(iii) Describe and explain what would happen to the spring in the forcemeter if Karen continued to add more mass to the forcemeter. (3)

(b) Copy and complete these sentences. (4)

Weight is a force caused by _____ acting on an object. _____ is not a force, and depends on the _____ and _____ of particles in an object.

(c) An astronaut working on the Space Shuttle can take a space walk and can move using four small jet motors attached to his space suit. This diagram shows the size and direction of four forces acting on the astronaut.

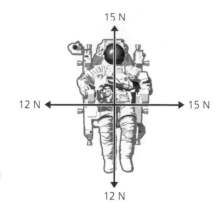

(i) The astronaut can move even though the forces produced by the jets are small. Explain why. (2)

(ii) Add an arrow to the picture of the astronaut to show the direction in which he would move. (1)

8 Rockets can be used to take astronauts into space. The diagram shows such a rocket shortly after take-off.

(a) The rocket is powered by burning a fuel load of liquid hydrogen and oxygen.

(i) Explain why the fuel is transported as liquids rather than as gases. (2)

(ii) Explain why oxygen is needed to burn the fuel, although vehicles do not need liquid oxygen when they transport the rockets around the launch sites on Earth. (1)

(b) (i) On the diagram, what are the two forces represented by the two arrows alongside the rocket? (2)

(ii) The graph below shows how the upward force and the weight of the rocket (including fuel) change during the first 40 seconds after ignition.

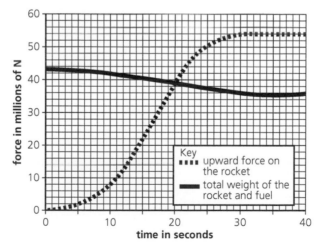

Use the graph to explain why the rocket cannot take off before 20 seconds have passed. (1)

(iii) What is the resultant force on the rocket after 30 seconds? Show your working. (2)

(iv) Why does the total weight of the rocket decrease during the first 30 seconds? (2)

9 This diagram shows the effect of a mass M on a spring.

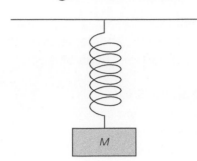

(a) Draw a diagram to show the effect of the same mass M on two identical springs joined in series (one after the other). (1)

(b) Draw a diagram to show the effect of the same mass M on two identical springs combined in parallel (one alongside the other). (1)

20 Friction, motion and pressure

1   Which option best completes each of the following sentences?

   (a) The strength of the turning effect of a force is a _____   (1)

   movement   moment

   leverage   rotator

   (b) A _____ is a simple machine that does **not** use the principle
       of levers _____   (1)

   crowbar   ski

   pliers   scissors

   (c) The unit for pressure is the _____   (1)

   newton   newton-metre

   newton per m²   foot-pound

   (d) Air resistance can also be called _____   (1)

   drag   pressure

   hindrance   thrust

   (e) The unit for moments is the _____   (1)

   newton

   foot-pound

   newton-metre

   newton per m²

   (f) The law of moments states that _____   (1)

   $\dfrac{\text{clockwise moments}}{\text{anti-clockwise moments}}$ is always less than 1

   clockwise moments + anti-clockwise moments = 1

   clockwise moments always exceed anti-clockwise moments

   clockwise moments = anti-clockwise moments

2 A farmer tried to pull out a tree stump by pulling with a rope.

■ Not to scale

(a) (i) The farmer attached a rope to the branch at point X, 0.5 m above the ground. He pulled with a force of 1000 N. Calculate the turning moment about the pivot point G. (2)

(ii) The farmer then attached a rope to branch Y, 0.8 m above the ground. What horizontal force would produce the same turning moment as before? (1)

(b) The tyres on the farmer's tractor have many grooves and ridges. Explain why this is important when working in a muddy field. (1)

(c) (i) Once the tree stump has been pulled out of the ground, the farmer decides to chop it up with an axe. The edge of the blade is sharpened so that it is very narrow. Explain why. (1)

(ii) The blade of the axe has an area of 1.2 cm², and the farmer can apply a force of 600 N. What pressure can the farmer exert on the tree? Show your working. (2)

3 Two pupils wanted to investigate friction between a surface and other materials. They used the apparatus shown in the diagram below.

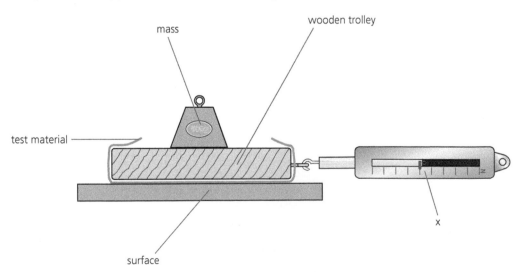

(a) (i) What is the name of the apparatus labelled X? (1)

(ii) Explain why it might be necessary to add the mass to the trolley. (1)

(b) In this investigation, what would be:

    (i)   the **input (independent) variable?** (1)

    (ii) the **outcome (dependent) variable?** (1)

    (iii) two **fixed (controlled) variables?** (2)

(c) Why should the pupils take three readings for each material? (1)

(d) The pupils obtained the following results:

Material	Test 1 (N)	Test 2 (N)	Test 3 (N)
P	2.0	2.0	2.0
Q	4.5	4.4	4.6
R	3.0	3.3	3.4
S	1.1	1.0	0.9
T	6.3	6.7	6.5

    (i)   Calculate the mean values for each of the materials. Give your answers to 1 decimal place. (2)

    (ii) Which material would be best for the soles of a rock climber's boots? (1)

    (iii) Which material would be best to rub onto the blades of a pair of ice skates? (1)

    (iv) What do you think would happen to the values for material R if the pupils polished the surface before they carried out the investigation? (1)

4   The diagram below shows a crane lifting a load. The crane has a movable counterweight.

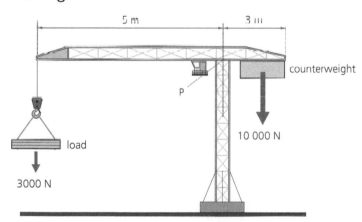

(a) Why does the crane need a counterweight? (1)

(b) (i)   What would be the turning moment of a 3000 N load about the pivot at P? (1)

    (ii) If the crane is balanced when a 4500 N load is being lifted, what moment must the 10 000 N force have? (1)

    (iii) How far from the pivot should the counterweight be placed? (1)

    (iv) What is the maximum load the crane should lift? (1)

5   Scientists have observed that in some parts of the world polar bears are interbreeding with grizzly bears. The hybrid animal is called a grolar bear! Look at this drawing of a polar bear.

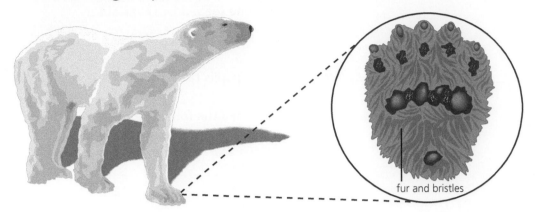

fur and bristles

(a) (i)   One difference between the two types of bear is that the true polar bear has much broader feet than the grizzly bear. How could these broad feet help the polar bear in its natural habitat, where it must walk across snowfields?   (2)

(ii) There is also another difference in the feet of the polar bear and the grizzly. The polar bear has many hairs on the soles of its feet, but the grizzly does not. Some of these hairs are short (like bristles), and some are more like fur. What are the advantages to the polar bear, in its natural habitat, of the **bristles** and of the **fur-like** hairs?   (2)

(b) Copy and complete the following sentences.   (2)

Inuit hunters who look for the polar bears rub fat and oil onto the

runners of their sledges. The oil acts as a _____ to reduce

_____ between the runners and the ice.

6   The diagram shows a siamang (a type of gibbon), hanging on a vine in a forest.

vine

2 m

(a) (i)   Would an arrow showing the direction of the siamang's weight point up or down?   (1)

(ii) Would an arrow showing the direction of the force of the vine on the siamang point up or down?   (1)

(b) The siamang can just reach the end of a branch of another tree. The branch is 2 m long, and the siamang has a mass of 12 kg. Calculate the turning moment applied when the siamang grabs the branch and lets go of the vine. Show your working. (2)

(c) The siamang is able to bite into the fruit because it has strong jaws. The diagram below shows how the animal uses its jaws to bite the fruit.

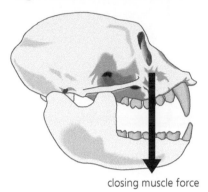

closing muscle force

    (i) The jaws work because there is a pivot in them. Draw two lines to represent the upper and lower jaws shown in the diagram, and label the pivot. (1)

    (ii) The siamang puts the fruit it is eating a long way from the pivot. Explain why this makes it easier to break open the fruit. (2)

7   Jack and Billy were going to build a model railway layout. They thought that they could glue a baseboard onto an old desk, even though the baseboard would overlap the desk by 50 cm. Their teacher thought the board would sag, and might even break, if they added any heavy items to it, and suggested that they carry out a test first. The diagram below shows the apparatus they used for their test.

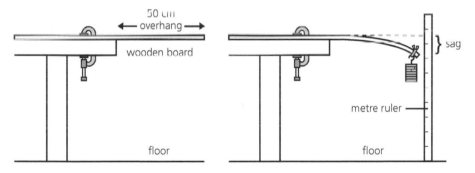

  (a) (i) Explain why their teacher thought that the board would sag or break. (2)

    (ii) The boys found that the board sagged by 1 cm even without any mass added to it. Why did this happen? (1)

(b) One part of the layout had a crane for adding boxes to trucks. The crane is shown in the diagram below.

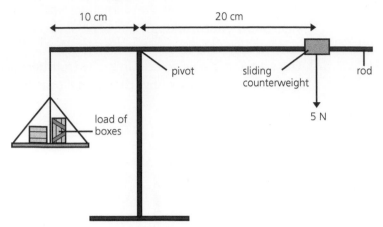

(i) Calculate the turning moment produced by the counterweight about the pivot when the crane arm is balanced horizontally. Give your answer in N m. (2)

(ii) Calculate the weight of the boxes. Show your working. (2)

(iii) Billy noticed that the loading crane did not always turn freely. Name one **substance** he could add to the pivot to help with this problem, and **explain** why it would work. (2)

21 Sound and hearing

1 Which option best completes each of the following sentences?

(a) The sound produced by a banjo string can be made louder by _____ (1)

using a thinner string   shortening the string

plucking the string harder   tightening the string

(b) Compared with light, sound travels _____ (1)

a little more slowly   much more slowly

much faster   a little faster

(c) The diagram shows the structure of the human ear.

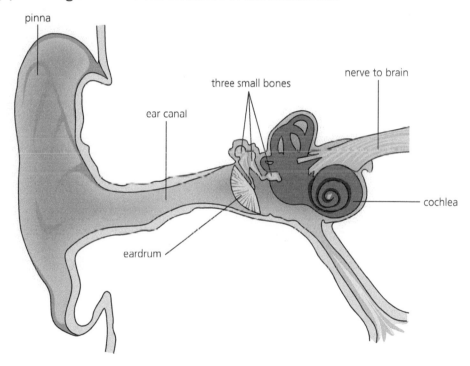

The first part of the human ear to vibrate when sound reaches it is the _____ (1)

cochlea   ear canal

pinna   eardrum

(d) Echo sounding is **not** used to _____ (1)

detect submarines   search for shoals of fish

listen to a message on the phone   locate sunken ships

(e) When an observer taps an aquarium, the speed of sound in the different parts is in the order (fastest to slowest) _____ (1)

glass wall – air – water – aluminium frame

aluminium frame – water – air – glass wall

air – water – aluminium frame – glass wall

glass wall – aluminium frame – water – air

(f) Sound _____ (1)

travels well through space   only travels through air

cannot travel through air   cannot travel through a vacuum

(g) The size of a vibration is its _____ (1)

pitch   amplitude

frequency   wavelength

(h) The frequency of a sound wave is measured in _____ (1)

joules   millimetres

hertz   millivolts

2   A teacher set up the piece of apparatus shown in the diagram.

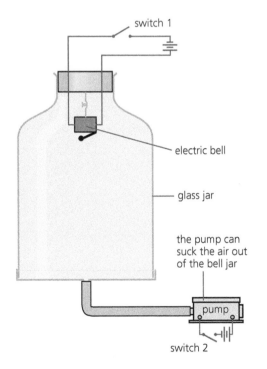

(a) (i)   Why can you hear the bell when switch 1 is closed? (1)

(ii)   What can you hear when switch 2 is closed? Explain your answer. (1)

(b) Annie was not paying attention to the teacher – she was looking out of the window. She saw two gardeners hammering in new fence posts around the hockey field. Annie saw one of the men hit the post with a sledgehammer. One second later she heard the sound.

(i)   Why did she hear the sound after she saw the hammer hit the post? (1)

(ii)   The gardener with the hammer moved halfway across the field, closer to the science laboratory. He started to hammer on another post. How long was the gap between Annie seeing him hit the post and her hearing the bang? (1)

there was no gap   longer than one second

less than one second   exactly one second

3 (a) The diagrams show the displays produced on an oscilloscope by four different sound waves.

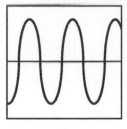 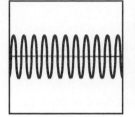 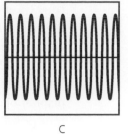 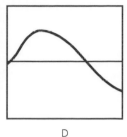

| A | B | C | D |

(i) Which **two** sounds have the same pitch? (1)

(ii) Which **two** sounds are as loud as one another? (1)

(b) (i) Builders using an electric drill might damage their ears. Explain how this could happen. (2)

The table below shows the maximum time that a builder can work with a drill at different sound levels without damage to his ears.

Sound level (decibels)	Maximum time in hours
86	8.0
88	4.0
90	2.0
92	1.0
94	0.5
96	0.25

(ii) What is the maximum time that the builder can work when drilling into concrete and making a sound of 89 decibels? Show your working. (2)

4 When the first astronauts landed on the Moon they were able to jump up and down, even though they wore heavy spacesuits.

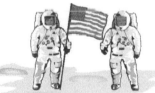

(a) (i) The astronauts were able to talk to each other and to the lunar craft because they had radios rather like mobile phones in their helmets. Without the phones they could not hear each other speaking. Explain why. (1)

(ii) The astronauts were told that if their phones broke down they could talk in an emergency as long as they touched their helmets together. Why could they hear each other when their helmets were touching? (2)

(b) (i) The astronauts were instructed to recharge their radio batteries when they returned to the spacecraft. The main batteries in the spacecraft were recharged using a freely available renewable source of energy on the Moon. Suggest what this renewable energy source is. (1)

(ii) Which energy transfer takes place in the radio battery as it is being charged? (1)

chemical to sound   thermal to electrical

sound to chemical   electrical to chemical

(c) The astronauts can tell when they are being called because they hear a buzz from the radio. The NASA technicians wanted to make sure that the buzz could be heard clearly. The diagrams show the display on an oscilloscope for four possible sound waves.

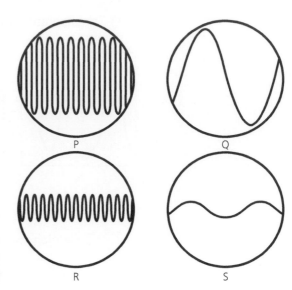

The scientists thought that a loud sound with a high pitch would be best. Which of the oscilloscope displays matches this requirement? (1)

5 Which option best completes each of the following sentences?

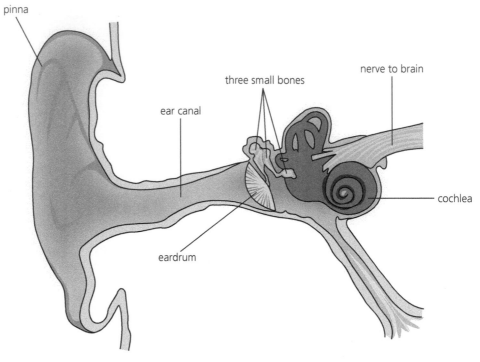

(a) Permanent deafness can occur if _____ (1)

the pinna is infected

the nerve to the brain is damaged

the eardrum is damaged by a pressure change

the ear canal is blocked by wax

(b) A violinist plays a note followed by one of lesser frequency. The first note will have sounded _____ (1)

softer   louder

lower   higher

6 The starter at the school Sports Day uses a starting gun with blank cartridges. He stands 5 m away from the starting line for each race.

(a) The starter wears ear defenders. Why does he do this? (1)

Physics

(b) Some senior pupils at the school were helping with the timing of the 200 m race. Each pupil was asked to record the time taken by a runner in a particular lane. One of them did not listen carefully to instructions, and started his stopwatch when he heard the bang from the gun and not when he saw the flash. Explain why the time he awarded to his runner would not have fitted in with the times awarded by the other pupil timers. (2)

(c) The diagram below shows where the running track was located. Some of the spectators in the seats labelled S thought that they heard two bangs at the start. Explain how this could have happened. (2)

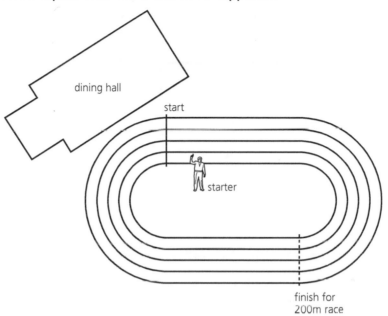

7 **(a)** The nerve in the ear carries messages about sound to the brain. To make this possible the ear transforms _____ (1)

light energy to electrical energy   electrical energy to sound energy

light energy to sound energy   sound energy to electrical energy

(b) The table below lists the range of frequencies that six different animals can hear.

Animal	Lowest frequency in Hz	Highest frequency in Hz
Human	30	20 000
Robin	300	30 000
Dog	30	45 000
Cat	20	65 000
Dolphin	80	125 000
Bat	2000	110 000

(i) A device sold by a pet shop is claimed to be able to frighten cats but not to affect dogs or birds such as robins. It does this by emitting a loud, high-pitched sound when a cat passes in front of it. Suggest and explain a suitable frequency for the sound emitted by the device. (2)

(ii) Dolphins find fish to eat by releasing short bursts of high-frequency sound. They work out how far away their prey is by measuring the time taken for an echo of the burst of sound to come back to them.

A dolphin emits a short sound burst and hears an echo 0.2 seconds later. Sound travels at about 1500 metres per second in salt water. Calculate the distance of the fish from the dolphin (show your working and include the correct units). (3)

8 David wanted to investigate which material would be the best sound insulator. He placed an electric bell inside a box, and then covered the box with each of the test materials in turn. The sound was detected by a sound sensor and recorded by a data logger, as shown in the diagram below.

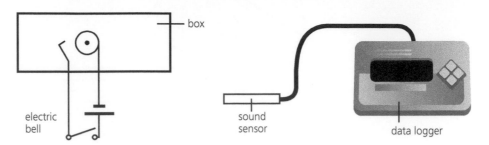

The results that David obtained are shown in the table below.

Insulating material	Sound level recorded
None	68
Paper	60
Polystyrene block	35
Cardboard	54
Cloth	48

(a) (i) Name the units for the sound level recorded. (1)

(ii) Draw a bar chart to represent these results. Use a graph grid like the one below. (4)

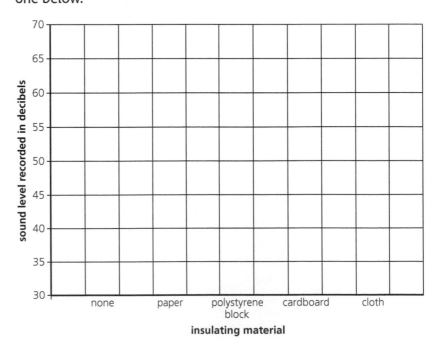

(iii) Which of the materials was the best as an insulator? (1)

(b) (i) For this investigation, name the **input** (independent) **variable**. (1)

(ii) Name the **outcome** (dependent) **variable**. (1)

(iii) Which of the following would have been **controlled variables** in his investigation? (2)

- the box used
- the distance between the sound sensor and the box
- the person who recorded the results in the table
- the light intensity in the room
- the time of the day when the results were obtained

Light

1   Which option best completes each of the following sentences?

(a) An example of a reflector and not a luminous source is _____ (1)

the Sun   a motorbike's headlights

the Moon   a Bunsen burner flame

(b) A material that does not allow light to pass through it
is _____ (1)

solid   transparent

opaque   a shadow

(c) Compared with a Formula 1 racing car, light travels _____ (1)

more slowly   much more quickly

at about the same speed   slightly more quickly

(d) Beams of light travel _____ (1)

at the same speed in every medium   in straight lines

at a speed that cannot be measured   as a single colour

(e) The image observed in a plane mirror is not _____ (1)

upright   back to front

the same size as the object   in front of the mirror

(f) When light is reflected from a plane mirror, the angle
of _____ (1)

incidence is greater than the angle of reflection

reflection is greater than the angle of incidence

incidence is equal to the angle of reflection

incidence is less than the angle of reflection

(g) The bouncing of light rays from a surface is _____ (1)

dispersion   reflection

refraction   diffraction

(h) Different colours of light are made of waves with _____ (1)

different frequencies   different densities

different amplitudes   different angles

(i) The splitting of light by a prism is _____ (1)

dispersion   reflection

refraction   diffraction

(j) A rainbow is caused by _____ (1)

light from our eyes being refracted by raindrops

sunlight reflected from the surface of water drops

sunlight being dispersed as it passes through water drops

sunlight reflected from the sky

2   Two students were interested in how shadows are formed and used the apparatus shown in this diagram.

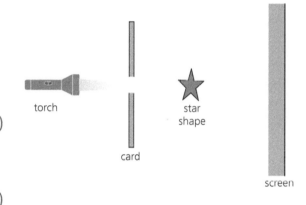

(a) Why must the card and the star shape be opaque?   (1)

(b) Draw two lines representing light rays to show how the shadow is formed.   (2)

(c) What would happen to the size of the shadow on the screen if the shape was moved further away from the card?   (1)

(d) Which word is used to describe a material that allows some light to pass through it?   (1)

3   Two mirrors held at 90° to each other always reflect a ray of light parallel to the incident ray.

(a) In this diagram, a ray of light strikes mirror A at an angle of 45°. Copy the diagram and then use a ruler and protractor to complete the diagram to show how the mirrors reflect the ray.   (2)

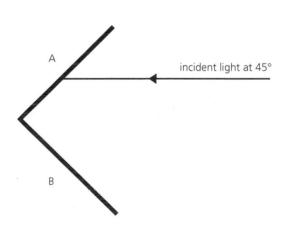

(b) In this diagram the source of light has been moved so that the ray of light strikes mirror A at a different angle. Copy the diagram and then use a ruler and protractor to complete the diagram to show how the mirrors reflect the ray. **(3)**

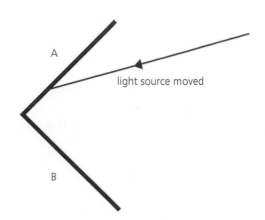

A

light source moved

B

(c) Policemen, ambulance workers and firefighters wear reflective jackets when working. The reflective stripes on the jackets are made up as shown in the diagram below.

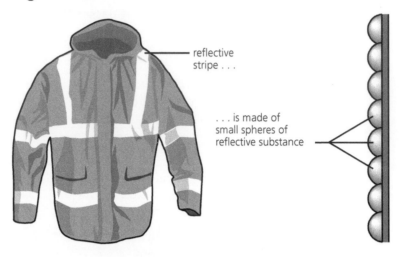

reflective stripe . . .

. . . is made of small spheres of reflective substance

(i) At night, road users can see these reflective jackets in the beam of their headlights. Explain why. **(2)**

(ii) Why would a plane mirror not be suitable for a reflective jacket? **(1)**

(iii) Explain why the cloth trousers of a firefighter (which do not have reflective stripes) do not give a clear reflection. **(1)**

4 The diagram below shows a ray of blue light passing through a perspex block.

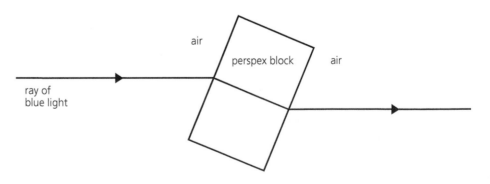

air

perspex block

air

ray of blue light

(a) As the light goes into the block it changes direction. What is the name of this effect? (1)

(b) The light leaving the block is not as bright as the light entering the block. Explain why. (1)

(c) Light can be made to pass through a prism, and to form a spectrum on a white screen.

Copy and complete this sequence to describe the colours of the spectrum. (4)

_____ _____ yellow _____

_____ _____ violet

5   At a zoo, the rare oomi bird had made a nest. The keepers at the zoo did not want to disturb the bird but wanted to allow visitors to view the nest. They built a piece of equipment like the one shown below.

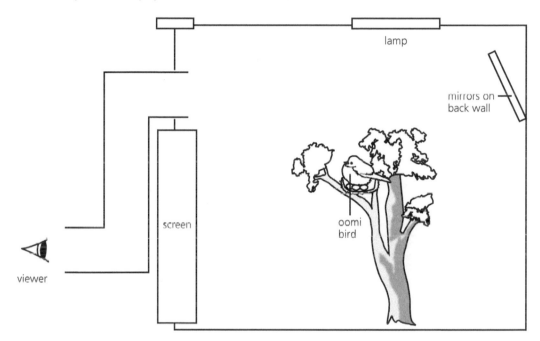

(a) Copy the diagram and add mirrors to show how the visitors would view the nest. (2)

(b) Draw a ray of light from the bird to show how it reaches the visitor's eye. Include arrows on the ray to show its direction. (1)

(c) Observers using binoculars for birdwatching hope to see a clear image. The most expensive binoculars have their lenses coated with a special material. The makers of the binoculars claim that this coating 'reduces dispersion'.

Explain why these expensive binoculars provide a more accurate coloured image than cheaper, non-coated, binoculars would do. (2)

6 A teacher uses a 'light
   pointer' to point at diagrams
   on the whiteboard. The
   pointer gives a very fine
   beam of red light.

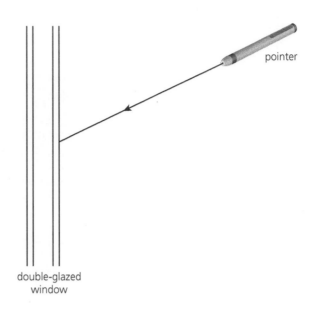

   If the teacher points the
   beam at a double glazed
   window the students can see
   two spots of red light.

   (a) Copy this diagram, then
       on the diagram:

       (i)   Draw the beam
             of light reflected
             off the first glass
             surface.   (1)

   double-glazed
   window

       (ii) Label the angle of reflection.   (1)

       (iii) Show how the beam is reflected to give the second red spot.   (2)

   (b) The beams are not as bright when they are reflected from the window
       as they are when reflected from a mirror. Explain why.   (2)

7 A snooker player is ready to play a shot, hitting the white ball against the blue.
   The table is well lit by a source of white light.

overhead light

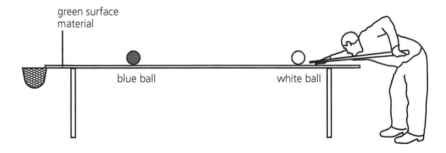

green surface
material

blue ball   white ball

   (a) Describe how light from the lamp lights up the balls and makes them
       visible to the player.   (2)

   (b) Which energy transformation takes place in the eyes to allow our brain to
       'see' an object?   (1)

   (c) If the overhead light stops working the players might use a light source
       from the side of the table. Explain why this causes shadows behind the
       snooker balls.   (1)

   (d) Light from the overhead lamp shines onto the snooker balls and onto
       the material of the table surface. Explain how reflection from the balls is
       different from scattering of light by the material of the table.   (2)

23 Electrical circuits

1   Which option best completes each of the following sentences?

    (a) A battery converts _____   (1)

       light energy into electrical energy

       chemical energy into electrical energy

       chemical energy into light energy

       electrical energy into kinetic energy

    (b) A chemical source of electrical energy is a _____   (1)

       terminal   cell

       fuse   transistor

    (c) A device that allows the flow of current in a circuit
       is a _____   (1)

       component   terminal

       switch   pole

    (d) The unit of electrical current is the _____   (1)

       amp   joule

       hertz   newton

    (e) A material that allows electricity to pass through it is _____   (1)

       an insulator   a circuit

       a cell   a conductor

    (f) A circuit with all of the components joined in a single loop
       is a _____   (1)

       parallel circuit   conducting circuit

       series circuit   short circuit

    (g) A component that can control the flow of a current
       is _____   (1)

       a resistor   a cell

       an ammeter   a motor

(h) Adding an extra cell to a series circuit that includes a lamp will make the lamp _____ (1)

fade   shine more brightly

shine as brightly as before   go cooler

(i) A circuit in which the current can only take one pathway is a _____ (1)

parallel circuit   switched circuit

series circuit   short circuit

2 (a) Link the correct name to each circuit symbol. Note that there are more names than symbols. (5)

Circuit symbol	Name
A 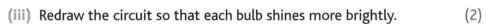	Ammeter
	Fuse
B	Switch
	Motor
C	Battery
D	Bulb
E	Resistor

(b) James made the circuit shown in the diagram.

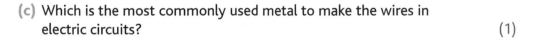

  (i) What is the energy source for the circuit? (1)

  (ii) Which component in the circuit is used to measure the current flow? (1)

  (iii) Redraw the circuit so that each bulb shines more brightly. (2)

(c) Which is the most commonly used metal to make the wires in electric circuits? (1)

3 The diagram shows a room heater used to warm up the gym on cold mornings.

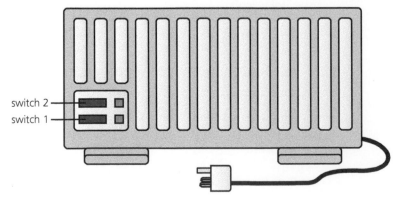

switch 2
switch 1

The school electrician had a diagram that showed the circuit for the heater.

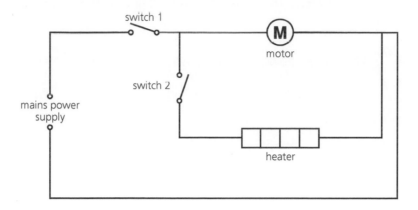

(a) (i)   Which switches must be closed for the heater to work?   (1)

   (ii)   Is it possible to have the heater on when the blower motor is
          switched off? Explain your answer.   (1)

   (iii) The heater and the motor are both on. A wire in the heater breaks.
          What effect will this have on the blower motor?   (1)

(b) Copy and complete this table to compare series and parallel circuits.   (4)

Feature	Series circuit	Parallel circuit
Value of current in different places		
Number of pathways that current can take		
Cost (higher, lower or the same) of operating components in the circuit		
Effect of one damaged component		

4 (a) The diagram below shows the parts of a cycle lamp.

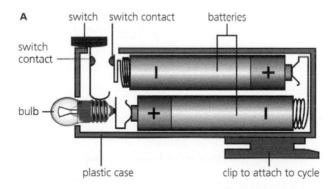

   (i)   Anna closed the switch. Why did this light the lamp?   (1)

   (ii)   Use the correct symbols to draw a circuit diagram for the lamp.   (3)

(b) Jamie borrowed the cycle lamp. The lamp would not light even when the switch was closed. The two diagrams show possible reasons for this.

B
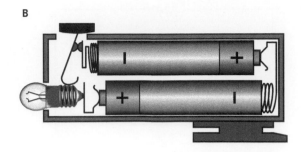

C
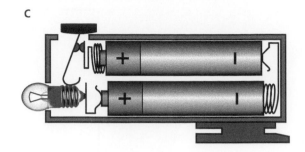

In each case, B and C, describe and explain what needs to be done to get the lamp to light. (4)

5 Janet and Imran were asked whether the thickness or the length of a piece of wire is more important in affecting its resistance. They were supplied with the following equipment:

- battery
- roll of thin copper wire
- switch
- roll of thin steel wire
- ammeter
- ruler with millimetre markings
- roll of thick copper wire

(a) Draw a circuit that they could use in their investigation. (2)

(b) For their investigation to be a fair test, identify the:

(i)   **input** (independent) **variable** (1)

(ii) **outcome** (dependent) **variable** (1)

(iii) **fixed** (controlled) **variables** (2)

(c) How could they try to make sure that their results were reliable? (1)

6 A teacher set up the circuit shown in this diagram.

(a) A current of 2.2 A flows through ammeter A3 when switch 1 and switch 2 are closed.

(i)   What will happen to each of the lamps when switch 1 is closed with switch 2 open? (1)

(ii) If ammeter A2 has a reading of 1.0 A when switch 1 and switch 2 are closed, what will be the reading on ammeter A1? (1)

(iii) What will be the reading on ammeter A1 if switch 1 is closed and switch 2 is open? (1)

(b) Complete the paragraph about electric circuits. Use words from this list. There are more words than spaces to be filled. (4)

buzzer	lamp
cell	lead
conductor	resistor
current	socket
filament	switch
insulator	

Electricity can pass through any material that is a _____. A complete circuit lets _____ flow all the way round it. The energy can be supplied by a _____ and can pass from one component to another through a _____. When a circuit is made up, it may include a _____, which can be opened to stop the flow of current. If the _____ is closed, then a component such as a _____ will light or a _____ will sound.

7 (a) A teacher was demonstrating circuits to her pupils. She built this circuit.

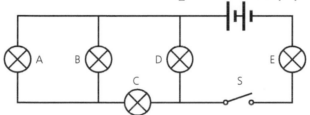

She closed the switch and all of the bulbs came on. One of the bulbs then failed and all of the bulbs went out. Which one of the bulbs must have failed? (1)

(b) The teacher then built a second circuit. She included a metal pencil sharpener and a plastic pencil sharpener in different parts of the circuit.

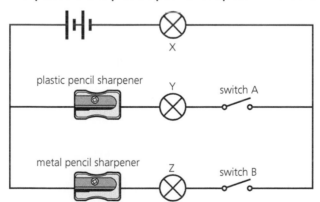

Copy and complete the table below to show which bulbs in this circuit will be **on** and which will be **off** when the switches are open or closed. (2)

Switch A	Switch B	Bulb X	Bulb Y	Bulb Z
Open	Open	Off	Off	Off
Closed	Open			
Open	Closed			

(c) Finally the teacher built this circuit, using a battery, three bulbs and four ammeters.

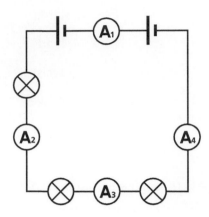

The current reading at ammeter A_1 was 0.6 amps. Which set of readings for the other ammeters, shown in the table below, is correct? (1)

Reading on A_2	Reading on A_3	Reading on A_4
0.2	0.2	0.2
0.3	0.0	0.3
0.6	0.6	0.6

 # Magnetic fields and electromagnetism

1 Which option best completes each of the following sentences?

(a) The ends of a magnet are called _____ (1)

   tips   terminals

   poles   fields

(b) An example of a metal that has magnetic properties is _____ (1)

   iron   copper

   tin   aluminium

(c) The rolled wire making up part of an electromagnet is the

_____ (1)

   coil   core

   turning   relay

(d) A compass needle shows the direction of the magnetic north pole because the compass needle is _____ (1)

   magnetised   a good conductor

   unmagnetised   heavier at one end

(e) The symbol for a relay is _____ (1)

   A   B   C   D

(f) A bar magnet has two poles, one north-seeking and one south-seeking. _____ will attract a piece of unmagnetised iron.

   both poles   only the north-seeking pole

   neither pole   only the south-seeking pole

2 (a) David is investigating the properties of magnets and wants to find a magnetic material. He has three pieces of metal – one is made of steel, one is made of tin and one is a magnet. He does not know which piece is which, but marks each one with a letter (X, Y or Z) and then uses a bar magnet to try to identify them.

He places the marked end of each piece of metal next to each pole of the bar magnet and writes down what happens in a table of results. Copy and complete this table of results. (3)

Test	Result	Conclusion
X [S | N]	Attracts	Metal X is
X [N | S]	Attracts	_____
Y [S | N]	_____	Metal Y is
Y [N | S]	Attracts	_____
Z [S | N]	_____	Metal Z is
Z [N | S]	Nothing happens	_____

(b) David took the piece of metal that was magnetised and laid it beneath a piece of card. He then sprinkled iron filings onto the card. Draw a diagram showing the pattern he would have seen. (2)

(c) David then took a small compass and placed it near to the magnet. Draw a diagram to show what would have happened to the compass. (1)

(d) Copy and complete this paragraph. (4)

When an unmagnetised iron nail is put into a _____ it becomes magnetised. The south-seeking pole of this nail will be _____ to the _____ pole of a bar magnet, but will be _____ by the north pole of the magnet.

3   A current flowing through a coiled wire acts like a magnet. The strength of this electromagnetic field can be increased by placing a core inside the coiled wire. A pupil decided to investigate the effect of the core material on the strength of the electromagnetic field. She used this apparatus.

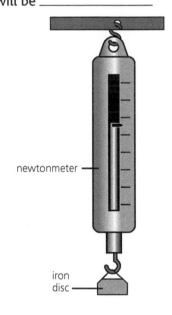

newtonmeter

iron disc

(a) Name three factors that should be kept constant to keep this as a fair test. (3)

(b) The pupil obtained the following results.

Material in core	Reading on newtonmeter in N
No core	1.4
Iron (no current)	1.0
Iron	1.8
Glass	
Steel	1.6

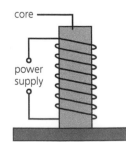

core

power supply

(i) Explain why the reading on the newtonmeter increases when a current passes through the coil. (2)

(ii) Suggest the likely value for the reading with glass as the core. (1)

4 Andy made two electromagnets, as shown below. The strength of the electromagnet was measured by how many paper clips could be picked up.

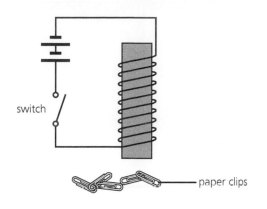

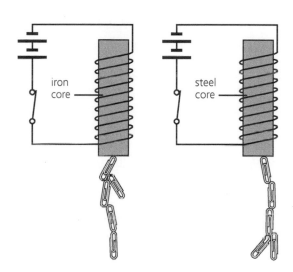

(a) (i) How can you tell that the strength of both electromagnets is the same? (1)

(ii) When the switches are opened the paper clips fall from the iron core but not from the steel core. Why is iron, rather than steel, used for the core of an electromagnet? (1)

(b) The diagram shows an electromagnet used in a scrapyard for separating different metals.

Explain how the electromagnet can separate the valuable aluminium from the less valuable iron and steel. (2)

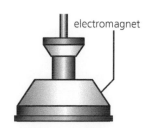

electromagnet

pile of metal:
mixed iron/steel/aluminium

(c) Some parts of the electromagnet crane are protected by circuit breakers. These automatically switch off a circuit if the current is too high. This diagram shows a simple circuit breaker.

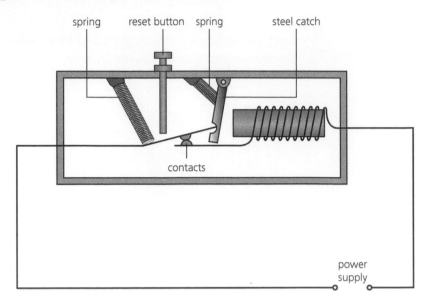

(i)   Explain why the current is cut off by this circuit breaker if it is larger than a certain value. (2)

(ii) Give **one** advantage of this type of circuit breaker compared with a simple electrical fuse. (1)

5   Which option best completes each of the following sentences?

(a) A magnetic field has _____ (1)

force but no direction   direction but no force

both force and direction   neither force nor direction

(b) An electromagnet can be made stronger by increasing the _____ (1)

diameter of the coil   length of time the current is passed

insulation on the wire   number of turns in the coil

(c) _____ does **not** use an electromagnet.

a relay   an electric bell

a compass   a DC motor

(d) The symbol for a reed switch is _____ (1)

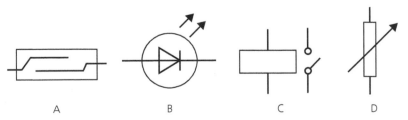

A   B   C   D

6 A reed switch is a small relay used in electronic circuits. It has thin metal contacts inside a glass tube.

(a) Jane set up the circuit shown below.

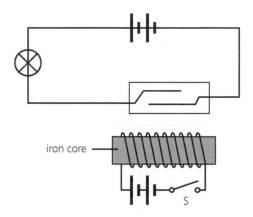

iron core

S

(i) She closed switch S but the lamp did not light. She knew that all of the connections had been made properly, and that the bulb was not broken. Explain why the lamp might not have lit. (2)

(ii) Suggest two things Jane could do to the electromagnet to overcome this problem. (2)

7 Saira used a sensor to measure the strength of an electromagnet. She placed the sensor 50 mm from the electromagnet and increased the current in the coil. She then turned the current down to zero, moved the sensor to 100 mm from the electromagnet and repeated the experiment.

The results are shown in the tables.

Sensor at 50 mm distance	
Current in amps	Sensor reading in N
0.5	0.35
1.0	0.68
1.5	1.00
2.0	1.30
2.5	1.50

Sensor at 100 mm distance	
Current in amps	Sensor reading in N
0.5	0.15
1.0	0.30
1.5	0.45
2.0	0.55
2.5	0.60

(a) Draw a graph of these results on a grid like the one below. (5)

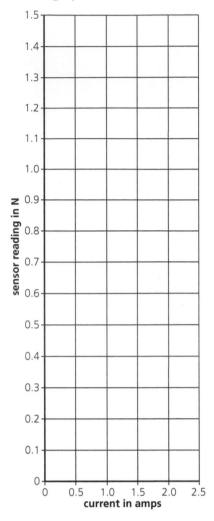

(b) (i) How did the size of the current in the coil affect the strength of the electromagnet? (1)

(ii) Suggest **two** other ways in which Saira could have altered the strength of the electromagnet. (2)

(c) An electromagnet can be used at a railway crossing barrier.

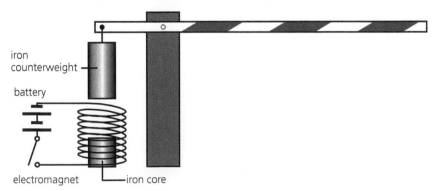

Explain how the electromagnet can be used to raise the barrier. (2)

8   The end of morning school is normally signalled by ringing an electric bell. The diagram shows the circuit for this bell.

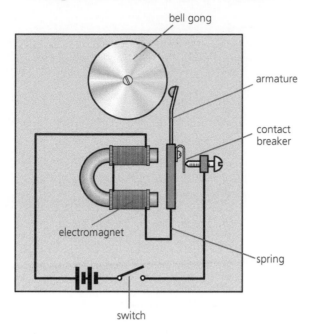

(a) The bell is normally silent. Explain why.   (2)

(b) Here is a list of possible actions in this circuit:

   • electromagnet pulls on armature

   • spring pushes armature back again so circuit is completed once again

   • switch is closed

   • contact breaker breaks circuit

   • armature moves so gong strikes bell

Write out, in the correct order, what happens to make the bell ring.   (5)

25 Space physics

1 Which option best completes each of the following sentences?

(a) On the Moon, gravity exerts a force of 1.6 N on 1 kg. An object that has a weight of 240 N on the Moon, has a mass of _____ (1)

400 kg	160 kg
150 kg	240 kg

(b) An eclipse of the Moon occurs when _____ (1)

the Sun lies between the Earth and the Moon

the Moon lies between the Sun and the Earth

the Moon is waning

the Earth lies between the Sun and the Moon

(c) The Sun is a _____ (1)

constellation	galaxy
star	planet

(d) The time taken for the Moon to complete one orbit of the Earth is a _____ (1)

year	day
lunar month	season

(e) We are sometimes able to see planets because _____ (1)

they are luminous

asteroids collide with the planet's surface

they reflect light from the Moon

they reflect light from the Sun

(f) _____ is the correct formula for the calculation of the weight of an object. (1)

$$\frac{mass}{gravitational\ field\ strength}$$ $mass^2 \times gravitational\ field\ strength$

$$\frac{gravitational\ field\ strength}{mass}$$ $mass \times gravitational\ field\ strength$

(g) The planet with an orbit closest to the orbit of the
Earth is _____ (1)

Uranus   Jupiter

Mercury   Venus

(h) Compared with sound, light travels _____ (1)

much slower   at the same speed

much faster   slightly faster

(i) The correct units for gravitational field strength are _____ (1)

kg per newton   newtons per g

newtons per kg   newtons per m

(j) Distances in space are so great that they are measured
in _____ (1)

millions of kilometres   sound years

light years   billions of kilometres

2   Copy and complete the following sentences. (5)

We are able to see stars because they are _____. Many stars seem

to be arranged in patterns called constellations and there may be several of

these in a single _____. The stars may be a great distance from the

Earth and may only be visible with an instrument called a _____

and we have to measure distances in _____. All the planets, stars,

gases and dust together make up the _____.

3   The diagram shows a satellite in orbit around the Earth.

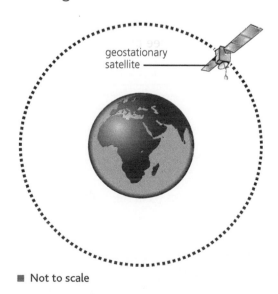

geostationary
satellite

■ Not to scale

(a) Copy the diagram and draw lines to show how a transmitter and receiver
would allow a football match to be seen in a different country. Do not worry
too much about drawing the countries accurately. (2)

(b) This type of satellite moves at a speed and height that means that it appears to remain in the same position relative to the surface of the Earth. It is called a geostationary satellite.

    (i) Why is it important for the satellite to remain in the same position above the Earth? (1)

    (ii) Once a TV satellite dish is fixed to the outside of a house, it does not need to be moved. Explain why. (1)

    (iii) How long does one complete orbit of a geostationary satellite take? (1)

    (iv) What is the force that keeps the satellite in position above the Earth? (1)

(c) Name **one** natural satellite of the Earth and **one** of the Sun. (2)

4 Copy the words in the boxes below and then draw lines to match each observation to the correct explanation. (5)

Observation		Explanation
1 year on Earth is 365 days		The Earth's axis is tilted
At the equator, there are 12 hours of light and 12 hours of darkness		The Moon orbits the Earth
In Britain there are four seasons in the year		The Earth orbits the Sun
There is a new Moon every month		The Earth is a sphere
A ship sailing away from land goes out of sight		The Earth rotates on its axis

5 This diagram shows a model of the solar system.

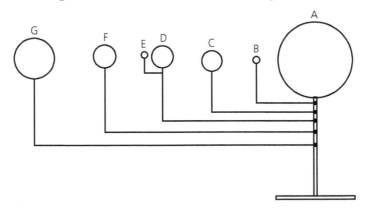

(a) Give the letter that is used to label:

    (i) the model Earth (1)

    (ii) the model planet that would be expected to have the highest surface temperature (1)

    (iii) a star (1)

(b) Spacecraft have allowed humans to stand on the surface of the Moon. This diagram shows an astronaut standing at four different positions on the Moon.

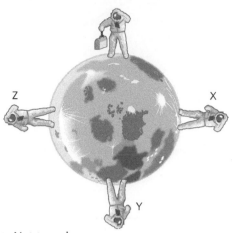

■ Not to scale

(i) Copy the diagram and draw an arrow at each of the four positions to show the direction of the force of the Moon's gravity on the astronaut. (1)

(ii) The astronaut is holding a bag for collecting samples on a chain. Draw the position of the bag in positions X, Y and Z. (1)

(c) The diagram shows that the Earth orbits the Sun.

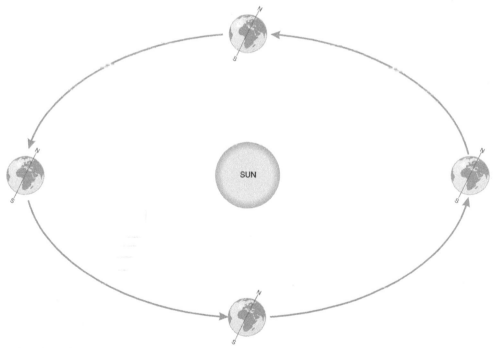

■ Not to scale

(i) Explain why the Earth orbits the Sun. (2)

(ii) How long does it take for the Earth to orbit the Sun once? (1)

(iii) Light travels at 300 000 km per second. The Sun is 149 million km from the Earth. How long does light take to reach the Earth from the Sun? Show your working. (2)

6   The diagram shows our solar system.

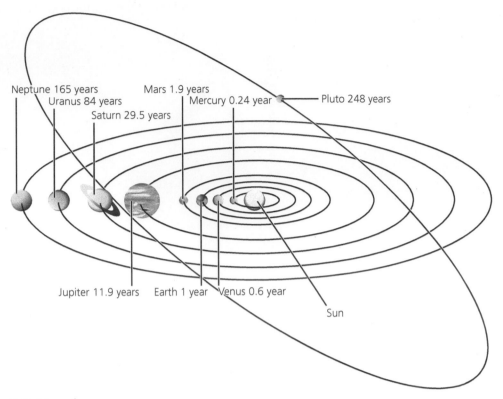

Neptune 165 years
Uranus 84 years
Saturn 29.5 years
Mars 1.9 years
Mercury 0.24 year
Pluto 248 years
Jupiter 11.9 years   Earth 1 year   Venus 0.6 year
Sun

■ Not to scale

(a) (i)   What evidence from the diagram supports the idea that Pluto is **not**
          a planet?   (1)

    (ii) The Hubble telescope has allowed astronomers to observe an object
          called Charon, which orbits Pluto. How does this support the idea
          that Pluto **is** a planet?   (1)

7   The diagram below shows the positions of the Earth, Moon and Sun during a
    lunar eclipse.

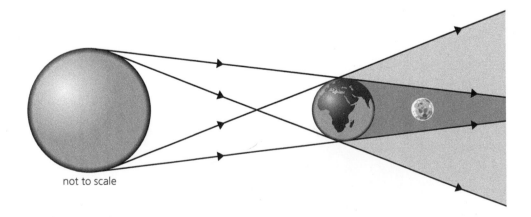

not to scale

(a) Redraw the diagram and add labels to **Sun, Moon, Earth** and **partial
    shadow.**   (2)

(b) Draw a second diagram showing the position of the Sun, Moon, Earth and
    complete shadow (umbra) during a solar eclipse. Label your diagram.   (3)

(c) A solar eclipse can upset the singing patterns of birds. Why do you
    think this is?   (1)